the Wonder of the His Name

32 Life-Changing Names of Jesus

MEDITATIONS BY

Nancy Leigh DeMoss

ARTWORK BY TIMOTHY BOTTS

Revive Our Hearts

Nancy Leigh DeMoss – General Editor

Timothy R. Botts – Calligraphy

Lydia Brownback – Devotional Editor

Dawn Wilson – Researcher

Lindsay Swartz – Researcher, Editorial Coordinator

Mindy Kroesche, Stacey Battenburg, Paula Hendricks, Kim Gwin – Editorial Assistants

Ben Hannah, Thomas A. Jones – Designers

Tom Mathis – Production Coordinator

Wes Ward – Revive Our Hearts Media Director

Mike Neises – Revive Our Hearts Publishing Director

ISBN 978-1-934718-43-8

Printed in the United States of America

Revive Our Hearts
P.O. Box 2000
Niles, MI 49120

Meditations based on the teaching of Nancy Leigh DeMoss: The Wonder of His Name

Revive Our Hearts radio series

Available at www.ReviveOurHearts.com/wonder

FROM MY HEART . . .

Names matter. Did you know that more than 350 names and titles related to Jesus can be found in the Scripture? The vastness of His character and His work on our behalf are revealed through His many names. The more deeply we explore the names of Jesus, the more we are able to move from simply knowing about Him to truly knowing *Him*.

This devotional, beautifully illustrated by renowned calligrapher Timothy Botts, is an invitation to experience "the wonder of His Name." My prayer is that these thirty-two meditations, along with the related hymns, quotes, and Scriptures, will draw you closer to our Savior and lead you to find fresh springs of grace and delight in Him.

May your heart be stirred as you fix your eyes on Jesus. And may you be transformed into more of His likeness as you behold Him in all His glory, humility, and love.

Nancy Leigh DeMoss

PS: You can learn more about the wonderful names of Jesus through the teaching series from which these devotionals have been drawn. The entire 32-part series is available for purchase on CD or MP3. Transcripts and audio are also available online at no charge. For more information, go to www.ReviveOurHearts.com/wonder.

4

Jesus! the Name high over all,
In hell or earth or sky;
Angels and men before it fall,
And devils fear and fly.

Jesus! the Name to sinners dear,
The Name to sinners giv'n;
It scatters all their guilty fear,
It turns their hell to Heav'n.

Jesus! the prisoner's fetters breaks,
And bruises Satan's head;
Power into strengthless souls it speaks,
And life into the dead.

Thee I shall constantly proclaim,
Though earth and hell oppose;
Bold to confess Thy glorious Name
Before a world of foes.

Happy, if with my latest breath
I may but gasp His Name,
Preach Him to all and cry in death,
"Behold, behold the Lamb!"

~ Charles Wesley
(1707–1788)

CONTENTS

"There is salvation in no one else, for there is no other name under heaven given among men by which we must be saved." ACTS 4:12

There is pardon
There is peace
There is power in the
Name of

Jesus

The Name above every name

8

"There is salvation in no one else, for there is no other name under heaven given among men by which we must be saved." (Acts 4:12)

The name *Jesus* was common in His day, yet this ordinary name became extraordinary, and down through history it has become unique. The reason for that is revealed in what the angel said to Joseph: "You shall call his name *Jesus*, for he will save his people from their sins" (Matt. 1:21). There has never been another *Jesus* like this one. His name reveals why He came to earth. It sums up His mission, His purpose, and His destiny.

Jesus is the Greek equivalent of the Old Testament Jewish name *Joshua*, which means "Jehovah saves." There were two Joshuas in the Old Testament. The first Joshua led the children of Israel from the wilderness into the Promised Land. He was a prototype of Jesus—a savior, a rescuer, a deliverer.

Our Joshua—Jesus—fights our battles. He has

conquered every enemy, including death, and He enables us to be victorious over temptation and sin. Our Joshua leads us into the spiritual inheritance that God has promised us, far surpassing the work of that first Joshua.

The other Old Testament Joshua was a high priest. God told the prophet Zechariah to make a crown of silver and gold and set it on the head of this Joshua (Zech. 6:11). God's instruction was a sign of royalty. Before this, the roles of king and priest had always been separate. Here, however, they are symbolically combined in one person. This is a wonderful picture of our Jesus, who is both King and Priest.

There is no other name like the name of Jesus. There is pardon in His name. By bearing our sins as His own on the cross and refusing to save Himself, Jesus has saved us from the penalty of sin and from the wrath of God, which we rightly deserve for our sins. He saves us daily from the power of sin. Jesus came not only to save us from the guilt and penalty of our sin, but also to take away our love for sin. And one day, we will be fully delivered from the very presence of sin.

There is power in His name. This name is what gives us access to God's greatest treasures. Of course, we know that the power is not in the name itself but in the Person who bears that name.

Jesus' name is precious. It is of infinite value. In fact, this common name became "the name that is above every name" (Phil. 2:9), and it is to be treated with great reverence.

"God has highly exalted him and bestowed on him the name that is above every name, so that at the name of Jesus every knee should bow, in heaven and on earth and under the earth, and every tongue confess that Jesus Christ is Lord, to the glory of God the Father" (Phil. 2:9–11).

Jesus! Name of wondrous love,
Human name of God above!
Pleading only this, we flee,
Helpless, O our God, to Thee.

- William W. How
(1823-1897)

"More than a great teacher, more than an enlightened man, more than a worker of miracles, more than a source of meaning in life, . . . more than a caring friend, more than a transformer of cultures, more than a purpose for the purposeless, Jesus is the Savior of sinners."[1]

- Kevin DeYoung

All hail the power of Jesus' name!
Let angels prostrate fall;
Bring forth the royal diadem,
And crown him Lord of all.

- Edward Perronet
(1726-1792)

"Jehovah saves"—that is the meaning of the name Jesus. In what ways have you experienced the deliverance promised in this name? Do you love, respect, and honor His name?

THE WORD

*In the beginning was the Word,
and the Word was with God, and the Word was God.
He was in the beginning with God. . . .
And the Word became flesh and dwelt among us. (John 1:1–2, 14)*

God is transcendent, and He dwells in unapproachable light (1 Tim. 6:16). It's impossible for us to see Him, much less draw near to Him, apart from Jesus. Jesus is God's mirror, and He came to earth to reveal God to man.

The apostle John tells us, "In the beginning was the Word, and the Word was with God, and the Word was God. . . . And the Word became flesh and dwelt among us, and we have seen His glory, glory as of the only Son from the Father, full of grace and truth" (John 1:1, 14).

John is the only New Testament author to call Jesus "the Word"—*Logos* in Greek. The Word has always existed, even before the heavens and the earth were created. John tells us that Jesus, the Word, is God. He became a man so we could see what God is like. He took on human flesh so God could be revealed to mankind.

Jesus is the physical manifestation of God the Father. He is the expression of the Father's thoughts, the Father's heart, and the Father's will. Jesus makes the invisible God visible. He makes the unknown God knowable.

He is also the means of communication between God and man. "For God, who said, 'Let light shine out of darkness,' has shone in our hearts to give the light of the knowledge of the glory of God in the face of Jesus Christ" (2 Cor. 4:6). Through Jesus, the transcendent, invisible, unknowable God draws near to us.

Jesus Christ, the living Word, was active in creation, and He holds together the world that He created. He has the whole world in His hands. The Word is active in redemption and in illumination. The Psalmist writes, "Your word is a lamp to my feet and a light to my path"

(Ps. 119:105). Our lamp is Jesus, the Word of God. He is the one who shines light on our steps.

Jesus is the eternal Word of the eternal God, the full and final revelation of God to all people. He will always be the personal, visible expression of the Father. Jesus did not come just to give us the Word of God—He is the Word of God. When Jesus speaks, God speaks.

Jesus reveals the way to the Father. He is God's final Word. He has spoken. Are we listening? Are we filling our minds with the world's novels, television programs, and music, or are we filling our minds with Jesus, the Word of God?

Because of Jesus, the *Logos*, we can know the Father. But we will never know the will of God, the thoughts of God, the mind of God, or the heart of God any better than we know His Son. If you want to know God, you must know Jesus. If you want direction for your life, listen to Jesus. Let Him speak to you through His Word.

"Unless a person expresses himself, his mind remains inscrutable. Similarly, God ordinarily would have remained beyond the comprehension of human beings. It became necessary for the Almighty to express Himself; in order to reveal Himself, He used the Word. Jesus became the channel of communication between God and human beings. . . . Jesus was the expressed eloquence and wisdom of the Most High God."[1]

- Ivor Powell

Ere the blue heav'ns were stretched abroad,
From everlasting was the Word:
With God he was; the Word of God,
And must divinely be adored.

- Isaac Watts
(1674–1748)

"In Christ, the revelation of God is complete and lacking in nothing."[2]

- Rubel Shelly

What does it mean to you to know that God desired to communicate to you through the living Word—His Son, Jesus? Jesus is revealed to us in the written Word, by the power of the Spirit. What steps are you taking to get to know God through His Son?

Son of God

*"The Holy Spirit will come upon you,
and the power of the Most High will overshadow you;
therefore the child to be born will be called holy—the Son of God."* (Luke 1:35)

Jesus is called the Son of God forty-seven times in the New Testament. He was declared by the Father to be the Son of God at His baptism and again at the transfiguration; even demons recognized Jesus as the Son of God. Jesus frequently referred to God as His Father, and in doing so, He was claiming to be God Himself—a claim that has caused no small controversy throughout church history.

As the Son of God, Jesus bears all of the divine nature. "He is the radiance of the glory of God and the exact imprint of [God's] nature" (Heb. 1:3). Jesus shares every attribute of God the Father equally.

The Father sent His Son to this earth to save us, but the Son was rejected by those He came to save. "He came to his own, and his own people did not receive him" (John 1:11), so they put the Son of God to death. But that was not the end of the story. The Father had the final word: "[Jesus] was declared to be the Son of God in power according to the Spirit of holiness by his resurrection from the dead" (Rom. 1:4). Forty days after the resurrection, the Son of God ascended back to heaven, and today the Son is seated at the right hand of the Father.

This is the Son of whom the Father says, "Your throne, O God, is forever and ever. . . . Sit at my right hand until I make your enemies a footstool for your feet" (Heb. 1:8, 13).

Psalm 2 tells us that the Son was given the kingdoms of the world as His inheritance. By His obedient life and death on the cross, Jesus won the right to rule over the nations. He won the right to judge and destroy those who rebel against Him and the right to save those who repent of their sins and believe on Him.

As the holy Son of God, Jesus perfectly loved, honored, and trusted His Father. When the Father sent Jesus to the world, Jesus fulfilled the Father's direction. When the Father sent Jesus to suffer and sacrifice His life for our sins, Jesus obeyed the will of the Father.

"For God so loved the world, that he gave his only Son, that whoever believes in him should not perish but have eternal life" (John 3:16). Oh, the wonder that, through believing in Jesus as the incarnate Son of God, we can have eternal life!

Do you love, honor, and trust your heavenly Father as Jesus did? Do you delight to obey the will of the Father? How do you respond when He sends you out to serve Him and sacrifice on behalf of others?

From God our heavenly Father
A blessed angel came;
And unto certain shepherds
Brought tiding of the same;
How that in Bethlehem was born
The Son of God by name.

- Traditional English carol

"We may well each one of us, cry out in astonishment, 'Lord, I ask no other sign, I want no further proof of Thy love. Now I know that Thou hast loved mankind with an everlasting love, seeing that Thou hast not withheld Thy Son, Thine only begotten Son Jesus, from us!'"

~ James Large

From Heav'n the Son of God descends,
And takes the form of Man.
To reconcile His foes as friends
Was all His gracious plan.

- A. W. Pickard-Cambridge
(1873-1952)

And the Spirit of the LORD shall rest upon him,
the Spirit of wisdom and understanding,
the Spirit of counsel and might,
the Spirit of knowledge and the fear of the LORD. ISAIAH 11:2

He is the Wonderful Counselor

Seek His counsel

Trust His counsel

Take His counsel

Son of man

But when the fullness of time had come, God sent forth his Son, born of woman, born under the law, to redeem those who were under the law, so that we might receive adoption as sons. (Galatians 4:4–5)

Have you ever considered that Jesus had a favorite title for Himself? Scripture seems to indicate that He did—"Son of Man." We find it eighty-four times in the Gospels alone, and the title shows us much about our Savior.

First, it shows us His humanity. Jesus had a physical body, which means He experienced hunger, thirst, weariness, grief, and temptation.

Also, the fact that He called Himself the "Son of Man" shows us His humility. How different we are from Him! We want people to know us by our most impressive title, yet Jesus chose His lowliest. The title speaks to us of why Jesus came: to seek, to save, to serve, and to give His life as a substitute for sinful man.

The title also speaks of His deity, His authority, His preexistence. Most frequently, the title

is used to speak of His future exaltation. When He returns to earth, He will come in power and glory.

The Son of God became the Son of Man so that the sons of men might become sons of God. Isn't that incredible? "See what kind of love the Father has given to us, that we should be called children of God; and so we are" (1 John 3:1).

As children of God, we are being made like Christ our brother. Slowly but surely we are taking on our eternal family resemblance. Our lives are increasingly marked by characteristics that were true of Jesus—humility, a heart to serve, and a willingness to suffer on behalf of others, as He suffered for us.

Son of God. Son of Man. The eternal destiny of every human being will be determined by their response to the

Son. The psalmist wrote, "Kiss the Son, lest he be angry, and you perish in the way, for his wrath is quickly kindled" (Ps. 2:12). This is none other than the Son of God—the King, the Messiah whom God has appointed to reign over the nations of the world.

In the ancient orient, kissing the hand or the robe of the king was a way to show homage. So to kiss the Son is a sign of subjection. It means to give Him our wholehearted allegiance. To kiss the Son is also a token of friendship. It is to draw near to Him and offer our worship, love, and affection.

Jesus came to earth the first time as the humble Son of Man, but when He comes the second time, He will come as God's instrument of judgment, and everyone who has refused to kiss the Son will perish eternally.

Psalm 2 ends with a word of resounding hope: "Blessed are all who take refuge in him" (v. 12). As you place your trust in Jesus, the holy Son of God, you can know that you are forgiven, and you can look forward to His return with great joy.

"He was God clothed in the garb of humanity. What unfathomable love! What condescension! That God should take upon Himself the frailty and the limitation of man. . . . The Infinite became Intimate."[1]

~ Henry Gariepy
(1930-2010)

"In this appealingly attractive title, Son of Man, we meet the merging of kingly strength and kindly sympathy. We also witness the blending of infinite power with intimate pity."[2]

~ Charles J. Rolls

Beautiful Savior! Lord of all nations!
Son of God and Son of Man!
Glory and honor, praise, adoration,
Now and forever more be Thine.

Have you experienced the blessing of taking refuge in Christ? If not, acknowledge that you deserve the wrath of God for your sins, and place your faith in the Son who bore God's wrath in your place.

Immanuel

"Behold, the virgin shall conceive and bear a son,
and shall call his name Immanuel." (Isaiah 7:14)

Isaiah encouraged Ahaz to ask for a sign of God's promise, but Ahaz didn't want a sign. He was unwilling to put his trust in the Lord. So Isaiah said to Ahaz, "Is it too little for you to weary men, that you weary my God also? Therefore the Lord himself will give you a sign. Behold, the virgin shall conceive and bear a son, and shall call his name Immanuel" (Isa. 7:13–14). God was going to give Ahaz a sign, whether or not he wanted one—not just for Ahaz's sake but also for the sake of God's covenant people.

This was a promise that the nation of Judah—in spite of its wicked king and the backslidden hearts of many of its people—would not be snuffed out, no matter how many threatening kings and nations surrounded them. A child named Immanuel would come to deliver, and they would have a glorious future, even though

things looked dismal at that moment.

Bible scholars differ as to the extent to which this prophecy was fulfilled in Ahaz's day. But we know that the prophecy found its ultimate fulfillment some 700 years later. The child born to Mary in Bethlehem was the one prophesied in Isaiah 7. In recounting the circumstances of Jesus' birth, Matthew tells us, "All this took place to fulfill what the Lord had spoken by the prophet: 'Behold, the virgin shall conceive and bear a son, and they shall call his name Immanuel' (which means, God with us)" (Matt. 1:22–23).

"I will be with you" is a promise found throughout God's Word. God with us—that is our greatest need in every circumstance, and God is with those who know and trust Jesus.

Immanuel, God with us, transforms ordinary moments and mundane tasks. If Jesus is your Immanuel, then in that profane work environment, God is with you. When you browse the Internet, God is with you. When your bills are greater than your income, God is with you. In that midnight feeding of a newborn, God is with you. At the graveside of a loved one, God is with you. When you are lonely, God is with you. When your heart is breaking, God is with you.

His presence can give you joy in the midst of every valley. When you don't know which direction to go, He is the guide for your journey.

If Jesus lives in you, then God is with you, and you can be free from fear. You can step out in faith, obey God, and fulfill His calling for your life. Immanuel is God with us for all of eternity.

"Jesus is the Eternal Immanuel—God with Us. . . . Through the indwelling Holy Spirit, Jesus is with his people personally, constantly, and forever."[1]

~ Rubel Shelly

"'Immanuel, God With Us.' Think of it! The Infinite an infant; the Ancient of days a child; the Ever-Blessed a man of sorrows and acquainted with grief! The idea is astounding, Divine!"[2]

~ C. H. Spurgeon
(1834-1892)

We sing, Immanuel, Thy praise,
Thou Prince of Life and Fount of grace,
Thou Flower of Heaven and Star of morn,
Thou Lord of lords, Thou virgin born.
Hallelujah!

~ Paul Gerhardt
(1607-1676)

God with us (Immanuel) is a miracle and an infinite blessing. What difference does His presence make in your life?

Wonderful Counselor

And the Spirit of the LORD shall rest upon him, the Spirit of
the Spirit of counsel and might, the Spirit of knowledge and the fear of the LORD. (Isaiah 11:2)

In the midst of dark days, Isaiah prophesied about the coming Messiah who would bring hope out of despair and light out of darkness: "For to us a child is born, to us a son is given; and the government shall be upon his shoulder, and his name shall be called Wonderful Counselor, Mighty God, Everlasting Father, Prince of Peace" (Isa. 9:6). Maybe you find yourself today in a dark place, wondering if God is really there, if He really cares.

He does care. He's the Wonderful Counselor. In Scripture the word *wonderful* is only used of God, never of man. Is He wonderful to you, or have you lost the wonder of who He is and what He has done? There are many good counselors in this world, but Jesus surpasses them all. What makes Him such a Wonderful Counselor?

He knows people. Jesus has insight into the human heart.

He knows our innermost thoughts and longings. Jesus knows us better than we know ourselves. He understands our needs because He has walked in our shoes, and He succeeded where we fail.

He is able to diagnose our problems. He can help us understand the root issues that need to be dealt with. It takes a great counselor to do that, and Jesus can do it perfectly.

He knows the right solution for our problems. He gives the counsel that is tailored to our specific situation. His counsel will always be consistent with His Word, and He knows whether we need encouragement, reproof, or practical instruction. He always knows what to do. This Wonderful Counselor knows everything. There is no limit to His knowledge and understanding.

He knows what we need to hear, even if we don't want

to hear it. He will tell us the truth about our real condition and the issues in our lives, if we'll listen to Him. The counsel of this world can actually make us worse instead of better, but Jesus' counsel will always make us better.

His counsel works. Think of the woman at the well who had a string of broken relationships. Jesus knew exactly what counsel she needed, and it changed her life. Think of the thief on the cross or the demonized man who lived in the tombs. Think of Nicodemus, the religious leader, who came to Jesus at night for counsel. Jesus gave each of them exactly the counsel they needed. And He counsels still today. I've seen Jesus heal hopelessly broken marriages. I've seen His counsel deliver people from sinful addictions.

Do you want to know God's will for your life? Do you want to know how to respond to your husband, how to raise your children, or how to deal with that difficult coworker? Are you facing a circumstance for which there seems to be no solution? Turn to the Wonderful Counselor; ask Him for wisdom, and then trust His counsel. He will never mislead you. "I bless the LORD who gives me counsel" (Ps. 16:7).

Where do you turn for counsel when you're desperate?
Do you try to advise Him, or do you ask Him to advise you?

"You and I need spiritual counsel, and Jesus Christ is perfectly qualified to be our Counselor."[1]

- Warren W. Wiersbe

"This Counselor is wonderful in His patience and love. ... There is no difficulty to intricate for Him to unravel. There is no little detail of life too petty for Him to take an interest in. ... There is no complication of difficult circumstances too extreme for Him to be willing to take hold of and lead us gently out into the light."[2]

- A. B. Simpson (1843-1919)

Every day, the Lord Himself is near me
With a special mercy for each hour;
All my cares He fain would bear, and cheer me,
He whose name is Counselor and Power.[3]

- Karolina W. Sandell-Berg (1832-1903)

"I have said these things to you, that in me you may have peace. In the world you will have tribulation. But take heart; I have overcome the world." JOHN 16:33

Peace can Reign in your heart No matter the situation Because you know the Prince of Peace

MIGHTY GOD

Lift up your heads, O gates!
And be lifted up, O ancient doors, that the King of glory may come in.
Who is this King of glory?
The LORD, strong and mighty, the LORD, mighty in battle! (Psalm 24:7–8)

The opening chapters of Isaiah's prophecy paint a dark and gloomy picture, but then comes a dramatic transformation: "For to us a child is born, to us a son is given . . . and his name shall be called . . . Mighty God" (Isa. 9:6). This promised child would be a powerful warrior. Christ is the fulfillment of this prophecy. He is the God who conquers, the God who prevails.

He is omnipotent. He has all power. He is able to bring joy and gladness and to transform gloom and anguish into joy. He is able to free His people from all their oppressors, no matter how powerful they might be. He has all the strength that is needed to intervene, to redeem, to deliver, and to save. Jesus is the Superhero of superheroes. He arrives on the scene and defeats those who oppress His people. *He is the Mighty God!*

It is astonishing that this Mighty God humbled Himself and became a helpless baby. He took on flesh and dwelt among us, and during this time He pulled back the curtain to show His might. He stilled storms, forgave sins, and healed diseases with a mere word or touch. He cast out demons and turned water into wine. He fed thousands with a boy's lunch. He raised the dead. *He is the Mighty God!*

Later, on the cross, Jesus conquered sin and Satan and hell and accomplished the mighty work of redemption. Then He threw off the shackles of death. He walked out of the tomb because *He is the Mighty God!*

That same Mighty God—the Lord Jesus—bears our burdens, supports us in our afflictions, and enables us to resist the power of temptation. He has delivered us from the penalty of sin and is delivering us from the power of sin. One day He will deliver us from the very presence of sin. He gives us strength to serve Him when we are weak and weary. He gives us the desire and power to obey Him when we are pulled by the world. *He is the Mighty God!*

He "breaks the power of canceled sin" in our lives. His power enables us to say "no" to sin and "yes" to God. It sets us free from the shame, guilt, and bondage of past sin. Jesus is mighty to preserve us from sin and Satan and self.

Nothing is too hard for Him—nothing! There is no one Jesus can't save. There is no heart so hard that He can't change it. *He is the Mighty God!*

"Whatever may be your burden or battle today, God has the power to meet it, handle it, solve it, and use it for your good and his glory. Jesus Christ is the 'Mighty God' and his power is available to you."[1]

– Warren W. Wiersbe

"Treasures of boundless might are stored in our Mighty God, and He dwells in the midst of His people; therefore may His people shout for joy."[2]

– C. H. Spurgeon
(1834–1892)

All hail, Thou Son of God,
    Mighty to Save;
Whose feet this earth have trod,
    Mighty to save;
We come to sing Thy praise,
Whose goodness crowns our days;
To Thee our anthems raise,
    Mighty to save.

– Rev. H. T. Zuley

Are you trying to carry burdens you're not strong enough to carry? Trust Him as the Mighty God in your life.

PRINCE OF PEACE

"I have said these things to you, that in me you may have peace.
In the world you will have tribulation.
But take heart; I have overcome the world." (John 16:33)

Every human heart longs for peace, but it's a gift that few experience. On the contrary, many of us are characterized by stress, fear, and anxiety. We lack peace in our relationships—we see conflict, tension, strife; we see divorce, church splits, and world wars.

It was into such a world that God sent an amazing gift. "To us a child is born, to us a son is given . . . and his name shall be called . . . Prince of Peace" (Isa. 9:6). The gift everyone wants—peace—is a Person. The Prince of Peace is God's gift to people who desperately need peace.

Jesus demonstrated extraordinary serenity under even the most intense pressure. We are easily stressed by the length of our to-do lists, but even though Jesus was given only about three years to accomplish God's eternal plan of redemption, we don't see Him being anxious, fretful,

or hurried. Things that make us hyperventilate didn't faze Jesus at all. He even slept in the back of a boat in the midst of a storm!

Jesus was peaceful in the face of constant criticism from the Pharisees. He maintained His peace when the fickle crowds screamed for His execution. Clearly, His peace did not come from the absence of problems. His peace came from His relationship with His heavenly Father. He knew everything was under God's control—the waves, the winds, the hungry people, and the Pharisees. He knew no one could do anything to Him apart from the Father's permission.

The first and greatest need in our lives is to have peace with God, and through Jesus' death on the cross, we can. This is the starting place for all peace. "But now in Christ Jesus you who once were far off have been brought near by the blood of Christ. For he himself is our peace" (Eph. 2:13–14).

Then, having received peace *with* God, we can have the peace of God. We can cease striving and be calm in the storms of life. We think, *Oh, if this problem would go away, I could be peaceful;* but peace is not the absence of problems. Peace is the presence of Christ in the midst of problems.

Because we live in a fallen, broken world, there will always be trials and disappointments. But in the midst of all of that, we can be at peace if we are rightly related to the Prince of Peace. It's a gift He gives as we trust Him.

You can't buy the peace you long for; you won't find it in a bottle, a pill, a trusted friend, or different circumstances. We experience peace when we rest in Jesus. If we focus on ourselves and our trials, we won't have peace. Peace was purchased by the Prince of Peace, and it's given to us as a gift. "Upon him was the chastisement that brought us peace, and with his wounds we are healed" (Isa. 53:5).

Do you have that peace, even though your circumstances today might be painful? The Prince of Peace will go with you where no one else can go. If you'll look to Him, He'll give you His peace.

Think of a time when Jesus brought peace into a tough circumstance you faced. Is there a situation you are facing today where you need His peace? Call out to the Prince of Peace.

"In the poor, decaying world, we have tribulations, trials, disappointments, sorrows of all kinds, but there never will be a time when we may not pillow our heads upon His shoulder and be at peace."[1]

– T. C. Horton &
Charles E. Hurlburt

"The same Cross that reconciles us to God also provides reconciliation with others, and the same Jesus who gives us peace with God is also the basis of our harmony with one another."[2]

– Robert J. Morgan

"The purchase of our peace was the sacrifice of himself, the ransom of his blood. . . . Without this, no sinner could ever hope for pardon, and all men must therefore have been for ever destitute of peace."[3]

– William Goode
(1762-1816)

Prince of peace, control my will;
Bid this struggling heart be still;
Bid my fears and doubtings cease:
Hush my spirit into peace.

– Charles Wesley
(1707-1788)

MESSIAH

He first found his own brother Simon and said to him,
"We have found the Messiah" (which means Christ). (John 1:41)

All through the Old Testament we find God's promise of a Messiah. In fact, there are hundreds of prophecies that give us glimpses and clues about Him. The word *messiah*, which means "anointed one," is the Old Testament counterpart to the New Testament term *Christ*.

This promised anointed one was to be supernaturally born in Bethlehem, a direct descendant of King David. He would perform miracles, heal the brokenhearted, and set captives free. And He would put an end to sin and bring in everlasting righteousness. There is only one person who fulfilled these hundreds of prophecies—Jesus. In so doing, He proved beyond the shadow of a doubt that He was the promised Messiah.

The Jews were waiting for God's Messiah, but under the oppression of the Romans, they developed an expectation that He would be a military hero sent to deliver them from political tyranny. When Jesus came, He acknowledged that He was, in fact, the promised Messiah, but His weapons were humble service, love, and ultimately His death. The Jews, however, had been expecting pomp and circumstance, and because He came quietly and without fanfare, they couldn't buy it. They thought it was scandalous that God's Anointed One would suffer, hang on a cross, and die.

By and large, the Jewish religious leaders rejected Jesus because they felt threatened by Him. They wanted to retain their power and control, yet Jesus was and is the Christ—God's Anointed One. Our culture seeks to debunk God's Word and tell us it isn't true, that we're nuts for believing an antiquated religious book. Doubts may arise in your own heart. But those doubts can be overcome as you renew your mind with the awesomeness of all those prophecies from the Old Testament that were fulfilled hundreds of years later in Jesus.

The fulfilled prophecies show us that God keeps His promises. He doesn't always do it in our way or time. Sometimes we have expectations of what Jesus should be like and of what He should do. We want to have the crown without the cross, and when He doesn't meet our expectations, we may be tempted to doubt that He really is the Lord.

The truth is, Christ's rule as our Messiah doesn't always lead to flamboyant victories or quick fixes. Sometimes His rule leads us through seasons of struggle, weakness, and hardship. But the hope to which we cling and the message we proclaim is that Jesus is the Christ, God's Anointed One, who came to deliver His people from sin and death.

The Old Testament prophesied that the Messiah would come, and He did—His name is Jesus. What does it mean to you that God keeps the promises He has made in His Word?

"Every Old Testament reference to the Messiah validates Christ's breathtaking claim, 'I am He.'"[1]

~ Henry Gariepy
(1930–2010)

I bless the Christ of God,
    I rest on love divine,
And with unfaltering lip and heart,
    I call the Savior mine.[2]

~ Horatius Bonar
(1808–1889)

"Jesus as Christ is the one in all of human history uniquely anointed and appointed to save."[3]

~ William D. Watley

"Behold, I am laying in Zion a stone, a cornerstone chosen and precious, and whoever believes in him will not be put to shame." 1 PETER 2:6

YOUR SALVATION DOESN'T REST ON YOU; IT RESTS ON CHRIST.

THE CHIEF CORNERSTONE

CHIEF CORNERSTONE

"Behold, I am laying in Zion a stone, a cornerstone chosen and precious, and whoever believes in him will not be put to shame." (1 Peter 2:6)

A cornerstone is the rock that makes a building stable. It is the most important stone, because it sets the course for the whole building. Jesus is the Cornerstone of His church—our solid Rock, our foundation.

The Psalmist wrote, "The stone which the builders rejected has become the chief cornerstone. This was the LORD's doing; it is marvelous in our eyes" (Ps. 118:22–23 NKJV). In the New Testament we learn that the builders in this psalm are the Jewish religious leaders—the scribes, the Pharisees, and the teachers of the law. They rejected Jesus. But God vindicated Him and established Him as the foundation of a new building that we know as the Church.

Nothing and no one can stop God's eternal purposes. God's plan for His people—God's plan for your life—cannot be thwarted. Others may oppose and reject you, but

God will have His way.

To those who believe and put their trust in this Cornerstone, that is a marvelous truth; but to those who do not, that Stone will be their undoing. Jesus said, "The one who falls on this stone will be broken to pieces; and when it falls on anyone, it will crush him" (Matt. 21:44). Jesus is in no way diminished by the rejection of those who don't believe in Him. Ultimately, they will be crushed.

There are only two possible responses to Jesus: reject Him or believe in Him. There's no middle ground. The apostle Peter calls Jesus "a living stone rejected by men but in the sight of God chosen and precious" (1 Pet. 2:4). *Is He precious to you?*

Peter continues, "You yourselves like living stones are being built up as a spiritual house, to be a holy priesthood, to offer spiritual sacrifices acceptable to God through Jesus Christ" (v. 5).

Through faith in Christ, we become living stones built on Him. We get a new identity. We're no longer defined by the failures of our past. Our identity is not found in our performance, our gifts, or our abilities. In Christ we're joined into a holy construction project—the building of a temple for God. This gives us hope when we're struggling to overcome a particular sin or trial.

The weight of the Church rests on Jesus and His finished work on the cross. Aren't you glad your salvation doesn't rest on you? He's the One who joins the whole building together. One day, when it's all finished, there will be a glorious, holy dwelling place for God. And in the meantime, we, as living stones, are safe and secure because we rest on Christ, our Cornerstone.

"The true Church is completely dependent upon the Lord who created it. Without the cornerstone, there would be no building; without the Chief Cornerstone, there would be no Church. Christians owe everything to their Savior."[1]

– Ivor Powell

"As you tell others about Christ, many will evaluate Him by the wrong standard and reject Him. Others will evaluate Him according to God's standard and find Him precious beyond measure."[2]

– John MacArthur

My hope is built on nothing less
Than Jesus' blood and righteousness.
I dare not trust the sweetest frame,
But wholly trust in Jesus' Name.
On Christ the solid Rock I stand,
All other ground is sinking sand.

– Edward Mote
(1797-1874)

How have you been comforted to know that Jesus is a Rock when the circumstances of life shift or fall apart? As the Cornerstone, Jesus provides stability and strength to His Church. Where do you need His stability and strength in your life?

For it was fitting for Him, for whom are all things and by whom are all things,
in bringing many sons to glory,
to make the captain of their salvation perfect through sufferings. (Hebrews 2:10 NKJV)

On June 11, 2001, as the infamous Timothy McVeigh was led to his execution, he handed the prison warden a note containing two lines from the Victorian poem "Invictus": "I am the master of my fate: I am the captain of my soul." This represents the mind-set of all who fail to acknowledge Christ as the *Captain* of their soul.

We first get a glimpse of our Captain in the Old Testament. As Joshua prepared to lead the Israelites into battle against Jericho, he had an encounter with a man who said to him: "I am the commander [captain, NASB] of the army of the LORD. Now I have come" (Josh. 5:14). This was likely a preincarnate appearance of the Lord Jesus—the Captain or Commander of the Lord's hosts.

A captain is a chief leader, a ruler, or a prince, and because the term is applied to Jesus, it tells us much about

Him. He is our head and our forerunner. As the Captain of our salvation, Jesus pioneered our faith. He provided the way to heaven. He took the lead to take us there.

Since Christ is our Captain, we must follow His marching orders, even when we can't understand what He's doing or we feel anxious about where He may lead us. If He is the Captain and we are His followers, then we owe Him our unquestioning loyalty and obedience. He can be trusted as our Commander. He looks out for His troops. He has given us the battle plan and leads the way forward. He is an able Captain and will not fail.

Knowing that Christ is the Captain of our salvation should strengthen and encourage us as we do battle against the world, the flesh, and the devil—all of which can seem overwhelming. But we can take courage as we realize that the greatest battle we will ever face—appeasing the wrath of God—was won for us at the cross by our Captain.

And He continues to fight for us now. He intercedes for us in heaven as we battle sin in our hearts and opposition from the world. We don't need to hide in shame, give way to despair, or cower in fear. Our mighty Commander is willing and able to resist the forces of evil in us, through us, and for us.

At the end of time, Jesus will come again, leading the armies of heaven to consummate the victory won on the cross and to cast down forever all the forces of darkness. This is our Commander. This is the Captain we will one day see with our eyes, as the King of glory comes to lead many sons to glory.

"We are called to conflict with the powers of darkness. But we have a glorious Captain that has gotten, and will give us, the victory over them."[1]

- Anne Dutton
(1692-1765)

"Do you not think that, sometimes, we act as if we had no Captain? We fancy that we have to fight our way to Heaven by the might of our own hand and by our own skill, but it is not so. Cast yourselves on your Captain's care. March onward though you cannot see your way! Be not afraid of anything, for your Captain is equal to all emergencies."[2]

- C. H. Spurgeon
(1834-1892)

Now let my soul arise,
And tread the tempter down;
My Captain leads you forth
To conquest and a crown;
A feeble saint shall win the day,
Though death and hell obstruct the way.[3]

- Isaac Watts
(1674-1748)

Jesus is our Captain, but we're not always faithful soldiers of the cross. What does it look like to be a good soldier? What is the difference between a spectator in the battle and one who follows hard after the Captain? Are you a soldier or a spectator?

friend of sinners

Now the tax collectors and sinners were all drawing near to hear him.
And the Pharisees and the scribes grumbled, saying,
"This man receives sinners and eats with them." (Luke 15:1–2)

Today we look at a name for Jesus that was, ironically, given to Him by His enemies. In derision and contempt the Pharisees called Him "a glutton and a drunkard, a friend of tax collectors and sinners" (Matt. 11:19).

Who were these tax collectors and sinners with whom Jesus ate? They were outcasts in Jewish society—the ceremonially unclean, money lenders, prostitutes, and those who made their living by ill-gotten gain. They were known to be morally questionable in some way. The Pharisees, on the other hand, were the ultra-religious people who prided themselves on not associating with sinners.

The Pharisees were shocked that Jesus would associate so freely with people who didn't live by the rules, and they demanded to know why He did. Jesus offered a powerful response: "Those who are well have no need of a physician, but those who are sick. I came not to call the righteous, but sinners" (Mark 2:17). Jesus came to heal those who were spiritually sick with the disease of sin. The Pharisees didn't realize that they were just as needy of spiritual healing as the sinners they so carefully avoided. They couldn't see their own spiritual need.

All through the Gospels we see that the Savior welcomed sinners and reached out to them, and sinners welcomed the Savior and responded to His outreach. That's an amazing picture of the very heart of redemption. It foreshadows the day when a multitude from every nation will sit together and eat with Him at the marriage supper of the Lamb.

God created us for companionship, but sin alienates us from God and from others. Jesus came to restore those broken relationships. As a friend, Jesus cared about people, regardless of their failures. He spent time with them and visited their homes. He got to know them.

Do you ever feel lonely, even in a crowd? I do sometimes. We have a constant friend in Jesus. Perhaps you identify with those sinners and you worry that if others really knew you, they'd shun you. Well, if you're that sinner (and who of us is not?), you have a friend in Jesus.

At the same time, we must remember that Jesus is not a friend of sin. He never condoned sin. To the contrary, He came to deliver sinners from their sin. Sin has to be paid for, and Jesus paid for it with His life. He is a friend to all who acknowledge their sin and will receive His friendship. And once you receive His friendship, you can't keep going on in your sin. His friendship is transformational. It will take away your desire for sin. Jesus associated with sinners so He could help them get well.

As sinners who have been befriended by Jesus, we should be known for welcoming and befriending other repentant sinners and for taking friendship and the gospel to them, even those we may not be comfortable with. Let's be faithful to introduce them to Jesus, the Friend of Sinners.

"I think in all the Bible, there is no sweeter name given to the Lord Jesus Christ than this. To think that those who are called the enemies of God have, for themselves, a Friend of such noble stature and quality as Jesus. He is the Friend of the friendless!"[1]

~ Alan Carr

"Laying aside the royal robes of Heaven, He came here to befriend sinful men. It was a life-work that cost Him His life. Hallelujah! What a Friend!"[2]

- T. C. Horton &
Charles E. Hurlburt

Jesus, the sinner's Friend, to Thee,
Lost and undone, for aid I flee,
Weary of earth, myself, and sin:
Open Thine arms, and take me in.

- Charles Wesley
(1707-1788)

What does it mean to you personally that Jesus is the Friend of Sinners? Do you have His heart for sinners who need to experience His redeeming love? What "kind" of people make you most uncomfortable—are you willing to befriend them in Jesus' name?

God said to Moses, "I AM WHO I AM." … Jesus said to them, "Truly, truly, I say to you, before Abraham was, I am." EXODUS 3:14; JOHN 8:58

IN JESUS CHRIST THE GREAT UNAPPROACHABLE I AM HAS DRAWN NEAR TO US

Jesus said to them, "Truly, truly, I say to you, before Abraham was, I am."
So they picked up stones to throw at him . . . . (John 8:58–59)

I n the Old Testament, God came to Moses and commissioned him to lead the Israelites out of slavery in Egypt, but Moses was hesitant; he said to God, "If I come to the people of Israel and . . . they ask me, 'What is his name?' what shall I say to them?" God replied, ". . . Say this to the people of Israel, 'I AM has sent me to you'" (Ex. 3:13–14).

God was revealing Himself as the self-existent One—self-reliant and self-sufficient. He is the uncreated Creator, the sustainer of all that exists. He is not dependent on anything or anyone. He is also unchanging and unchangeable. God is never altered by circumstances outside of Himself. Nothing arises that He hasn't thought of or planned for. He never gets caught off-guard. He is the same yesterday, today, and forever.

When Jesus came to earth, He made an astonishing claim—to be the great I AM. The God who delivered His people from captivity in Egypt was still alive and at work in human history! In fact, He had entered human history in the flesh!

The Pharisees accused Jesus of having a demon, but Jesus responded: "Your father Abraham rejoiced that he would see my day. He saw it and was glad." The Jews were incredulous: 'You are not yet fifty years old, and have you seen Abraham?' Jesus said to them, 'Truly, truly, I say to you, before Abraham was, I am'" (John 8:56–58). The Jews were outraged because they understood exactly what Jesus meant. He was claiming to be Yahweh, the great I AM who had revealed His name to Moses.

Therefore, to reject Jesus is to reject God. Everything

that's true of God is true of Jesus. Jesus has all the attributes of God: He is self-existent, self-sufficient, unchanging, and eternal. He always was and always will be. Jesus came to reveal God to us. In Jesus Christ, the great unapproachable I AM has drawn near to us.

Jesus does the works of God. As Jehovah delivered His people out of slavery in Egypt, Jesus delivers and sets captives free. He has rescued us from slavery to the ultimate Pharaoh—Satan—and sin. And He continues to rescue us from ourselves, from the power of sin, and from the entanglements of this world.

As Jehovah led His people into the Promised Land in the Old Testament, so Jesus came to lead many sons to glory. He leads us today by His Spirit, who lives in us. As God promised to be with Moses, Jesus is with us today. He will enable you to do whatever He calls you to do.

Jesus gives us Himself to fill up whatever we need or lack. Do you have a thirsty soul? He is living water. Do you have a hungry heart? He is the bread of life. Do you feel the weight of sin? He is the resurrection and the life. Do you feel lost? He is the way. Jesus says, "I am all that you need. I am the great I AM."

"We are introduced to One in the midst of mankind who is able to transform water into wine, translate from darkness to light, and transfigure death into life, who is none other than the great I AM. . . . I AM meets every need of the human race."[1]

~ Charles J. Rolls

"He was the Eternal Son of God. He was the Uncreated One, the Eternal One, the Self-existent one. Before the creation of the world, He was the 'I Am!' After the world passes away He will still be the 'I Am.'"[2]

~ T.C. Horton &
Charles E. Hurlburt

Behold Him there, the risen Lamb,
My perfect, spotless Righteousness
The great unchangeable I AM,
The King of glory and of grace.[3]

~ Charitie Lees Bancroft
(1841-1923)

Over and over again, Jesus proved His character and power as Jehovah, the great I AM. We can trust Him to help us in times of need. What needs are you looking to Jesus to meet, trusting Him to care for you?

*"I am the bread of life; whoever comes to me shall not hunger,
and whoever believes in me shall never thirst."* (John 6:35)

In ancient times, bread was vital for life. That perspective of bread as a basic necessity is reflected when we call money "bread" or "dough." In Scripture, bread is an object lesson for our basic spiritual needs; it also points to God's provision for those needs, His presence to fill and sustain us.

In John 6, Jesus performed a miracle with bread, feeding a hungry crowd from just five barley loaves and two fish. After the crowd ate their fill, there were twelve baskets of bread left over. The next day Jesus addressed that crowd and said, "Truly, truly, I say to you, you are seeking me, not because you saw signs, but because you ate your fill of the loaves" (v. 26).

The people in the crowd were following Jesus for the miracles. They were curious but not converted. They were impressed with Jesus but not ready to invest their lives in Him. They wanted Jesus for what they could get from Him.

Where do you turn for fulfillment? Earthly things—even good things—don't last. Jesus made that point to the crowd, and then He said, "I am the bread of life; whoever comes to me shall not hunger, and whoever believes in me shall never thirst. But I said to you that you have seen me and yet do not believe" (vv. 35–36). Jesus was claiming to be the one and only source and sustainer of life.

Not everyone in the crowd was happy to hear Jesus' claim. Many grumbled and refused to believe—they were angered by Jesus' insistence that He is the only way to have life. But Jesus didn't back down. He never tames His claims for those who don't believe. You may not believe in Him, but He is still the Bread of Life.

If you eat this Bread, you live forever. If you don't eat this Bread, you will die. It's a matter of life and death. The essence of sin is that we want to rely on something or someone other than Jesus. If we want to live, we must eat of Christ, the Bread of Life, which means that we come to Him and cease relying on ourselves.

You've heard it said, "You are what you eat." Well, as we feed on Jesus in His Word, we become like Him. We're changed into His likeness. If you gorge on "junk food," you're not going to have much appetite for the true Bread of Life. Jesus and His Word will seem boring. Do you hunger for Jesus? To come to Him in faith is to recognize your desperate daily need for Him.

In order for us to have eternal life, Jesus, the Bread of Life, had to die. At the Last Supper, "Jesus took bread, and after blessing it broke it and gave it to the disciples, and said, 'Take, eat; this is my body'" (Matt. 26:26). His body was about to be broken on Calvary so the hunger of the world could be satisfied.

Oh, that we would cease seeking fullness in things that can't give us life! Christ is the Bread from heaven—the One who eternally satisfies our souls.

Are you hungry for the Bread of Life? What are some of the "junk foods" that can dampen our appetite for Christ, the true Bread?

"[Jesus] is a heaven-sent source of everything we need to remain inwardly and eternally healthy."[1]

– Robert J. Morgan

"Only Christ, who is the Bread of Life, can satisfy the deepest hunger and yearning of the soul."[2]

– Henry Gariepy
(1930–2010)

"You must not just have that bread in front of you in the gospel and be able to say how good it looks and how sweet it smells to your spiritual sight and taste. You must eat it. You must appropriate Christ and assimilate Him in your heart and soul. You must take Him in and digest Him as the very food for your soul."[3]

– Rev. Charles Terpstra
(1924-2004)

"Those who are full are not interested in food. In the same way, sinners who are satiated with their sin have no hunger for spiritual things."[4]

– John MacArthur

The people dwelling in darkness have seen a great light, and for those dwelling in the region and shadow of death, on them a light has dawned. (Matthew 4:16)

Truth, goodness, holiness, purity, godliness—Scripture intertwines each of these with light. God's presence is associated with light, and His Word is said to be light. It makes sense, then, that sin and death have to do with darkness. Ever since sin came into the world, mankind has lived in darkness. We stumble around unable to see truth and beauty. But all through the Old Testament a great light was promised, a light that would come and push back the darkness.

During the Feast of Tabernacles, an annual event celebrated by the Jews, a ceremony took place called the Illumination of the Temple. Every night during the feast, four young men would climb ladders to fill four golden lamp bowls with oil and to light giant, seventy-five-foot-tall candelabras. The light lit up the temple, poured over the temple walls, and lit up the whole city. It reminded the

people of that great light promised by the prophet Isaiah for those who walk in darkness.

John 8 records a dramatic scene that took place on the day after this ceremony was celebrated, while the memory of the lights was still fresh in everyone's minds. Jesus boldly proclaimed, "I am the light of the world. Whoever follows me will not walk in darkness, but will have the light of life" (John 8:12).

He was saying that the light of the temple, though truly magnificent, inevitably sputters out; but those who believe and follow Him will never walk in darkness. "I have come into the world as light," He said, "so that whoever believes in me may not remain in darkness" (John 12:46).

Light reveals what the darkness conceals, and Jesus came to reveal God to us. His light also reveals our hearts and our sinfulness. His Word is a lamp to our feet and a light to our path (Ps. 119:105). It guides us and reveals obstacles and pitfalls in the way.

Light is more powerful than darkness. In fact, it dispels darkness. Darkness has no power over light. When you turn on the light, darkness flees. For centuries people have tried to extinguish the light of God's Word and of Jesus. Our world remains in moral and spiritual darkness. We are confronted with injustice, oppression, hopelessness, despair, cruelty, moral insanity, hatred, and broken lives. There's darkness in our own hearts, as well.

But Light has come into the world. Jesus is the "star out of Jacob" (Num. 24:17), the "sun of righteousness" (Mal. 4:2), the "bright morning star" (Rev. 22:16), and the "Sunrise from on high" (Luke 1:78 NASB). One day He will return, and there will be a final great sunrise—the new Jerusalem "has no need of sun or moon to shine on it, for the glory of God gives it light, and its lamp is the Lamb" (Rev. 21:23).

Can you imagine it? No more darkness. No more night. Only eternal, brilliant, glorious Light. His name is Jesus. In the meantime, He lives in us and shines through us into our dark world.

Jesus' light drives out darkness, but it also reveals things hidden in the darkness. Are there any "hidden" things you need to bring to Jesus today? Any dark places in your heart that need to be brought into His light?

"The world without Christ is a world of darkness, groping and lost. . . . He alone can save man from the deep and dark night of sin."

– Henry Gariepy
(1930–2010)

"Jesus being 'the light of the world' means the world has no other light than him. If there is going to be a light for the world, it will be Jesus. It is Jesus or darkness. There is no third alternative. No other light. . . . All the world, and everyone in it, needs Jesus as their light."[2]

– John Piper

The whole world was lost
In the darkness of sin;
The Light of the world is Jesus!
Like sunshine at noonday,
His glory shone in.
The Light of the world is Jesus!
Come to the light, 'tis shining for thee;
Sweetly the light has dawned upon me.
Once I was blind, but now I can see:
The Light of the world is Jesus!

– Philip P. Bliss
(1838–1876)

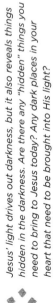

"I am the bread of life; whoever comes to me shall not hunger, and whoever believes in me shall never thirst." JOHN 6:35

As we partake of food to sustain our bodies, so we must partake of Christ, the Bread of Life to feed our souls each day

Good Shepherd

For the Lamb in the midst of the throne will be their shepherd,
and he will guide them to springs of living water. (Revelation 7:17)

Sheep can't fend for themselves, which is why they need a shepherd. In truth, we're not much different than sheep—shepherding is necessary for our survival. So what a joy when we realize that God has always been the Shepherd of His people, both collectively and individually. We find His shepherding all through the Old Testament, and yet there is also the promise of a Shepherd to come, one who will lead and guide His flock.

That Shepherd did come! His name is Jesus. He says, "I am the good shepherd. I know my own and my own know me . . . and I lay down my life for the sheep" (John 10:14–15). Jesus is again claiming to be Jehovah.

As the Shepherd, He owns the sheep. They belong to Him, and He knows them. Our Good Shepherd has a personal relationship with His sheep—a warm, intimate, caring relationship. We can be in a crowd and feel unknown, but in Jesus' fold, we don't get lost among the flock. He knows each of us by name. He knows our background, our tendencies, and our vulnerabilities. He knows where we're tempted and tested, and He knows our needs.

This Good Shepherd leads His sheep. He goes before them. He knows the terrain, and He can lead them through the most difficult places.

The Old Testament tells us about unfaithful human shepherds—religious leaders who were supposed to feed the sheep but fed themselves instead. They cared nothing for the sheep. By contrast, the Good Shepherd loves the sheep. Aren't you glad we have a good, faithful Shepherd?

Unfaithful shepherds abandon the sheep when there's danger, but the Good Shepherd stays with the sheep when no matter what. He never leaves them, especially when there's danger. There are times we may feel abandoned by God, but the truth is that He will never abandon us.

Unfaithful shepherds are out for what they can get, but the Good Shepherd is a giver. Unfaithful shepherds are self-seeking, but the Good Shepherd is self-sacrificing. Unfaithful shepherds come to steal, kill, and destroy, but the Good Shepherd came to give life.

Are you looking to Jesus to shepherd you? Are you part of His flock? If so, He will always be your Shepherd—comforting, guiding, and providing—and you will echo the Psalmist who says, "The LORD is my shepherd; I shall not want" (Ps. 23:1).

"Shepherd. Implied in that simple word is a promise: everything a shepherd was to his sheep, the Lord is to me. He leads me, feeds me, tends to my needs and comforts me. He even bears me up in His arms as needed."[1]

– Robert J. Morgan

"Jesus is still the King and the Shepherd of his people. He is still enthroned in heaven, watching over his flock."[2]

– Charles Degner

Savior, like a shepherd lead us,
Much we need thy tender care;
In thy pleasant pastures feed us,
For our use thy folds prepare.
Blessed Jesus, blessed Jesus!
Thou hast bought us, thine we are.

– Dorothy A. Thrupp
(1779–1847)

Reflect on what it means to have Jesus as your Shepherd. How does this encourage you today? Can you trace how your Good Shepherd has led you in "paths of righteousness"?

Resurrection and the Life

"Fear not, I am the first and the last, and the living one. I died, and behold I am alive forevermore, and I have the keys of Death and Hades." (Revelation 1:17–18)

Ever since the Fall, death has been an inevitable and painful part of life (Gen. 2:17; Rom. 5:12). Sooner or later, we all taste the grief it brings and face it ourselves.

In the Gospel of John, we find death confronting a close-knit family in the village of Bethany. Lazarus had died, and four days after his death, Jesus arrived on the scene. He said to Martha, Lazarus' grieving sister, "Your brother will rise again" (John 11:23).

Martha knew that Jesus could raise her brother from the dead someday, but she needed faith for her present situation. Jesus knew that and assured her, "I am the resurrection and the life. Whoever believes in me, though he die, yet shall he live, and everyone who lives and believes in me shall never die" (v. 25–26).

Jesus told Martha not only what He would do but also who He is. Life is wrapped up in Jesus. There is no physical life apart from God, and there is no spiritual life apart from Jesus. The resurrection is not just an event—it is a Person. Jesus is the answer to death!

"Do you believe this?" Jesus said to Martha. "Do you believe in Me? Do you believe that I am who I say I am?" Believing in Him is a matter of life or death. Martha replied, "Yes, Lord; I believe that you are the Christ, the Son of God, who is coming into the world" (v. 27). At that moment, faith overcame her confusion and despair.

What about you? Do you believe that Jesus is who He claimed to be? Do you believe that those who die believing in Jesus have eternal life?

Jesus went to the grave of Lazarus with Martha and her sister Mary, where He demonstrated His power.

He declared His authority over life and death, saying, "Lazarus, come out" (v. 43). And Lazarus came walking out of that tomb!

Jesus gives abundant, eternal life to those who place their trust in Him. He delivers from fear of death. He brings hope where there would otherwise be only despair. In Jesus, death is not final.

At the funeral of my youngest brother, David, who had been killed in a car accident, one of the ministers said, "We think of David as having gone from the land of the living to the land of the dead, but the fact is, David has gone from the land of the dying to the land of the living." That is the truth, for those who believe in Jesus, the Resurrection and the Life.

He came to redeem not just our souls, but our bodies, as well. Every part and particle of our beings will one day share in His resurrection life. He "will transform our lowly body to be like his glorious body" (Phil. 3:21). This is all bound up in the fact that Jesus is the Resurrection and the Life.

Knowing Jesus as the Resurrection and the Life can infuse life into hopeless situations where there is no life. Breathe on us, Spirit of Jesus!

> "If Jesus were still in His borrowed tomb, we'd be helpless and hopeless. But because of His resurrection, we have hope today and every day."[1]
>
> – David Jeremiah

> "He has triumphed over the power of Satan in the soul of every sinner who believes in Him—He shall triumph in their bodies also."[2]
>
> ~ J. N. Darby
> (1800–1882)

> "Jesus raised Lazarus because he is the resurrection. He is the arrival in history of God's final, glorious renovation of all things, including our bodies. Believers, you will be raised from the dead and shine like the sun in the kingdom of your Father. Lazarus is a preview of your resurrection."[3]
>
> ~ John Piper

How does knowing Jesus as the Resurrection and the Life give you hope in the present? How does it give you hope for your future? How does it affect our perspective on death?

#

"For this purpose I have come into the world—to bear witness to the truth. Everyone who is of the truth listens to my voice." (John 18:37)

As I listen to my piano tuner at work, adjusting each note to a fixed pitch, I can't help but think how a fixed standard of truth has been largely discarded in our day. Individuals have their own truth. People are tuning their instruments to whatever pitch they happen to like, and the result has been confusion and chaos.

It has become increasingly difficult to convince people that Jesus is the absolute, unchanging standard of truth. But that's what He claimed to be. And that's what He is.

God is true to His Word and His promises. He is faithful, reliable, and trustworthy. There is no deception or hypocrisy in God. He is the fixed standard of truth. And that truthful character of God establishes the standard for all of mankind. It's an absolute standard, one from which there is no deviation, and it's absolutely required for

anyone who wants to have fellowship with Him. If we're off pitch, then we cannot walk in one accord with God.

Now that obviously creates a problem, because every human being enters this world off pitch. Because we are sinful, we don't meet God's standard. We twist the truth. We lie to ourselves, to others, and to God.

Jesus is the only person who has ever perfectly fulfilled God's standard of truth. Jesus is God's "fixed pitch" against which all other pitches must be calibrated. Jesus said to Thomas, "I am the way, and the truth, and the life. No one comes to the Father except through me" (John 14:6). Jesus doesn't just say that He is speaking truth; He says He *is* the Truth.

Anything that is out of alignment with Jesus is not truth, no matter how true you might think it to be. Your attitude toward truth will be exactly the same as your attitude toward Jesus, because truth and Jesus are inseparable. Your attitude toward one reveals your attitude toward the other. If you reject the truth, you will reject Jesus. If you love the truth, you will love Jesus.

Our culture considers it intolerant to insist on a "fixed pitch" that all else must be tuned to, but many so-called believers fall into this trap, too. There's a tendency today to pit truth against qualities such as love, mercy, and grace, and truth seems to lose out in some circles. But truth is not incompatible with love, mercy, and grace.

God's truth is never at the expense of mercy, and His mercy is never at the expense of truth. Both are epitomized in Jesus. The psalmist says, "Mercy and truth have met together" (Ps. 85:10 NKJV). That happened at the cross, where Jesus gave His life for fallen sinners.

We don't have to apologize for saying that Jesus is the Truth. Those who know it are called to be faithful witnesses, pointing people to Him with grace and mercy. Eternity is at stake. That Day is coming when the one whose name is Faithful and True will return to earth, and every knee will bow and every tongue confess that Jesus is exactly who He claimed to be.

"Jesus Christ is the Faithful and True Witness. He doesn't waver in His resolve or forget the promises He's made. He will never disappoint. He isn't fickle, but always faithful, the same yesterday, today, and forever. Keep your eyes on Him."[1]

– Robert J. Morgan

"In His response to our search for truth, Christ does not give us a precept but a Person; not a what, but a who; not a code or a creed, but His own character. . . . Jesus reveals to us the truth about God, ourselves, and our world."[2]

– Henry Gariepy
(1930–2010)

Jesus, my Way, my Truth, my Life,
My God, my All in all;
At Thy blest feet, in humble love,
And lowly fear, I fall.[3]

– William Mason
(1725–1797)

What are some of the voices of "truth" in the culture that many people believe and follow? What voice of truth do you follow, and what difference does that make in how you live?

"I am the good shepherd. The good shepherd lays down his life for the sheep." JOHN 10:11

The Good Shepherd is attentive to your needs and knows how to meet them, He cares for you!

We have seen and testify that the Father
has sent his Son to be the Savior of the world. (1 John 4:14)

Television news commentators spend countless hours debating what will bring change to our society, but we rarely hear any mention that the greatest need of the human race is salvation. Ever since the Fall, all of mankind has been in desperate need of deliverance. We need a Savior—one who delivers.

A savior rescues, heals, and preserves—and He has come. Our Savior is Jesus. Saving sinners is His mission, "for the Son of Man came to seek and to save the lost" (Luke 19:10).

It's important to know your need of this Savior; if you don't, then you will never embrace Him. My childhood home burned the night before I started my sophomore year of high school. My family was deeply grateful for the rescue workers who came to save us from the fire—we

knew we needed to be rescued!

The wrath of God is a far worse fate than any earthly disaster. Jesus came to save us from divine judgment. Either you will have salvation through Jesus Christ, or you will experience the eternal wrath and judgment of a holy God because of your sin.

Salvation or wrath—there's no middle ground. There's little teaching today on the holiness and the wrath of God, so people have no sense of the danger. The fact is, we deserve to be damned eternally, and if He does not save us, we must bear our own judgment.

There is salvation in no one but Jesus, "for there is no other name under heaven given among men by which we must be saved" (Acts 4:12). You cannot be saved by looking anywhere else for deliverance.

Jesus also saves us from darkness. "He has delivered us from the domain of darkness and transferred us to the kingdom of his beloved Son" (Col. 1:13). So often we think of our salvation as a moment in time. We make a profession or a decision, we pray a little prayer, and then we go right on with our lives. What a travesty!

Let's not miss the grand sweep, the full extent, of God's amazing salvation. He came to save us, every part of us, from all the consequences of the Fall. Jesus came to melt our hard hearts, to give us the gift of repentance, and to take away our love of sinning.

And Jesus is "able to save to the uttermost" (Heb. 7:25)—completely, every part of us, for all time, no matter who we are or what we've done. Jesus can save the most resistant, hard-hearted sinner.

He was sent to save; He is able to save; He is willing to save; He is mighty to save. Do you need to be saved today? If so, turn your eyes upon Jesus. Call out to Him from your heart right now.

"Remember what you were and would have become without a Savior. Remember! Remember!"[1]

– John Piper

"Jesus is a greater Savior than you think him to be when your thoughts are at the greatest."[2]

– C. H. Spurgeon (1834-1892)

Jesus, Savior, Son of God,
Bearer of the sinner's load,
Breaker of the captive's chain,
Cleanser of the guilty's stain.

Savior, Surety, Lamb of God,
Thou hast bought us with Thy blood;
Thou hast wiped the debt away,
Nothing left for us to pay.

– Bickersteth's Christian Psalmody (1833)

What does it mean to you (past, present, and future tense) to know Jesus as your Savior?

LORD

Thomas answered him, "My Lord and my God!" (John 20:28)

In our individualized Western culture, we are resistant to thinking of anyone or anything being "lord" over us. We don't want someone telling us what to do. Yet the offer of salvation throughout Scripture is never separated from the call to turn from sin and self and to follow Christ and bow to His authority.

"Lord" is not just a title—it's a name that carries with it authority and the right to rule. It represents a mandate to obey God and to declare with our hearts, our lips, and our lives, "Jesus is Lord!"

But there's something in the way—our sin. Underlying all sin is the desire to be our own lord. Confessing and calling on Jesus as Lord represents a complete change of mind and heart. It means repenting from calling the shots in our own life and from doing what we want to do when

we want to do it.

Repentance is turning from ourselves as lord and bowing before Jesus, apart from which there is no true salvation. "If you confess with your mouth that Jesus is Lord and believe in your heart that God raised him from the dead, you will be saved" (Rom. 10:9).

Jesus is our Lord and Savior, and those titles are inseparable. Someone who professes to be a Christian but gives no credible evidence of following Christ as Lord, no evidence of a changed heart and life, can have no basis for assurance of salvation. Certainly change is slow, and the path forward seems difficult sometimes. There are occasions when we give in to the drives of our flesh. But someone who stays in that place and experiences no conviction of the Holy Spirit and no repentance, likely does not have a saving relationship with Christ.

There is a huge difference between giving lip service to Jesus as "Lord" and truly knowing Him as Lord. Jesus said, "Not everyone who says to me, 'Lord, Lord,' will enter the kingdom of heaven, but the one who does the will of my Father who is in heaven" (Matt. 7:21).

On another occasion, He said, "Why do you call me 'Lord, Lord,' and not do what I tell you?" (Luke 6:46). Jesus then paints a picture of the destruction that comes upon those who don't submit to His lordship. You can claim to know Jesus, but that's not necessarily proof of genuine faith. True faith will always be demonstrated in a life that desires to obey God.

If Jesus is God (and He is), then He must be Lord. He is supreme. We are not our own; we belong to Him. That's the truth about Jesus as Lord. But we're not talking about some onerous obligation. There is infinite grace wrapped up in His lordship! He is a compassionate Lord. He always does what's best for His subjects. We can surrender our lives to Him without fear.

As the psalmist reminds us, "Since he is your [Lord], bow to him" (Ps. 45:11).

"What makes this universe a cosmos, rather than a chaos, is that the Lord Jesus Christ is holding it all together. . . . Jesus is Lord! That is what we believe, . . . that is what we proclaim to the world. There is no Christianity apart from this."[1]

– D. Martyn Lloyd-Jones
(1899-1981)

"When the early Christians chose to say, 'Jesus is Lord' as their declaration, they were literally choosing to align everything with Jesus, even their own lives. . . . Those three words changed everything."[2]

– Ed Stetzer

"No one has any right to believe that he is indeed a Christian unless he is humbly seeking to obey the teachings of the One whom he calls Lord."[3]

– A. W. Tozer
(1897-1963)

As others observe your daily life, would they conclude that Jesus is your Lord? Is there any area of your life where you are reserving the right to be your own lord? What would it look like to surrender that area to Jesus' control?

And he put all things under his feet and gave him as head over all things to the church. (Ephesians 1:22)

A head and a body: that's an important metaphor Paul uses to describe the relationship between Christ and believers: "He is before all things, and in him all things hold together. And he is the head of the body, the church. He is the beginning, the firstborn from the dead, that in everything He might be preeminent" (Col. 1:17–18).

From a physiological standpoint, a head and a body are organically united. Just so, Jesus is organically, inseparably connected to His Body, the Church. The Church is not an institution; it is a living organism. A body cannot exist apart from the head, and in the same way, the Church derives its life from its Head, Christ. We have no life apart from Him, and those who are not connected to Him are dead, spiritually speaking.

Walking, talking, swallowing, breathing, and

thinking—all these functions are controlled by the brain, which is in the head. The brain controls emotions, memory, and perception. The brain sends out signals to other parts of the body and governs all it does.

As the Head of the Church, Jesus is the "brain"—the control center for every function of His Body. He rules over His Church. He knows what every member of the Body needs, and He supplies those needs.

Every member of the body has a direct relationship with the head. That's why Paul says that we must hold fast to Christ. If we have a right relationship with our Head, then we will have a right relationship with other members of the Body. The Body can't function unless the individual members are connected to each other and all the members together are connected to the Head.

Paul wrote, "I want you to understand that the head of every man is Christ, the head of a wife is her husband, and the head of Christ is God" (1 Cor. 11:3). Christ is the Head of His Church, but He also has a Head. The Father and the Son are equal with each other, yet the Son is subordinate to the headship of the Father—joyfully so.

Watching Jesus take His place under the headship of the Father shows us the beauty of God's created order. Being under headship isn't a burden—it's a privilege! As our Head, Jesus cares for us and always acts in our best interests. He protects us and provides all we need to sustain life.

Everything about your Christian life hinges on your connection to Christ, your living Head. We were created to glorify Him, and that happens as we rightly respond to Him. Have you acknowledged Christ as your Head? Are you conscious that you cannot live without Him?

One day, at the end of time, all things will be placed in subjection under the headship of Christ, and He will reign forever and ever.

"The church does not exist apart from Christ, her Head. The Church is defined in terms of its relation to Christ."

– John MacArthur

"In the true Church of God, Jesus Christ is the great directing Head; from Him the only binding commands go forth; to Him all the really spiritual yield a cheerful homage; his members delight to do the will of their Head."[2]

– C. H. Spurgeon
(1834–1892)

Head of the church triumphant,
    We bring our adoration;
Till you appear, your servants here
    Shall sing with great elation:
We lift our hearts and voices,
    With blest anticipation,
And cry aloud to you our God
    The praise of our salvation.

– Charles Wesley
(1707–1788, adapted)

What privileges or blessings do those in the Body of Christ receive from being connected to Christ, our Head? What are some implications for how we "do church"?

We have seen and testify that the Father has sent his Son to be the Savior of the world. 1 JOHN 4:14

We cannot save ourselves
We need a Rescuer, a Deliverer, a SAVIOR

Great High Priest

Since then we have a great high priest who has passed through the heavens,
Jesus, the Son of God, let us hold fast our confession. (Hebrews 4:14)

Before Christ came, priests were a vital part of life for God's people. They were needed because of sin. Sinful people cannot approach a holy God directly, so God in His mercy appointed priests to serve as mediators. These priests offered prayers and praise on behalf of the people, and they offered sacrifices for their sins. The priests represented all the needs of the people to God, and they represented the grace and the mercy of God to the people.

The high priest ranked above all other priests. On the Day of Atonement he would kill the sacrificial animals; then he would go into the Most Holy Place and sprinkle the blood of the slain sacrifice on the mercy seat. In this way, atonement was made. The wrath of God was satisfied, and God's mercy was extended to His people once again.

But like the people they represented, the priests were sinful. They had to offer sacrifices for their own sins before they could offer sacrifices for the people. Only Jesus meets our need for a perfect high priest, and He had to become a man to fulfill that office. "He had to be made like his brothers in every respect, so that he might become a merciful and faithful high priest in the service of God, to make propitiation for the sins of the people" (Heb. 2:17).

Those earlier priests held only a temporary priesthood because, at some point, they died. But Jesus' priesthood is permanent. It's eternal because He lives forever. There's no need for any other priest to ever take His place.

The Old Testament priests had to offer sacrifices daily, but Jesus' sacrifice of His life was sufficient once for all, which is why He cried out from the cross, "It is finished!" The animals sacrificed under the old covenant merely foreshadowed the one future sacrifice that would fully atone for sin. As the perfect Lamb of God, Jesus offered Himself—the perfect sacrifice for every sin. He is both sacrifice and priest.

The Old Testament priests entered the presence of God in the temple once a year, but when Jesus offered His perfect sacrifice for sin, the veil that separated the Most Holy Place from the rest of the temple was torn in two from top to bottom, thereby opening the way of access to God. The barrier is gone, so now we can come with confidence into the very presence of God.

And, praise be to God, Jesus' priestly work on our behalf is not over! He intercedes for us in heaven. Our Great High Priest is "able to save to the uttermost those who draw near to God through him, since he always lives to make intercession for them" (Heb. 7:25).

As we cry out to Jesus, He sympathizes and understands, and He makes intercession for us to the Father. We don't have to worry that God might reject us for something we did. We can go with confidence in the name of Jesus, because the price for our sin has been paid.

Are you burdened with a load of guilt? Do you have concerns that seem too heavy to bear? If you know Christ as your Great High Priest, draw near to the throne of grace, and there you will receive mercy and find grace to help in time of need.

"We are saved eternally by the eternal prayers and advocacy of Jesus in heaven as our high priest. He prays for us and his prayers are answered because he prays perfectly on the basis of his perfect sacrifice."[1]

– John Piper

"Satan may condemn us, but our great High Priest holds forth His pierced hands, and that is enough."[2]

– T. C. Horton &
Charles E. Hurlburt

Jesus, my great High Priest,
Offered His blood and died;
My guilty conscience seeks
No sacrifice beside.
His powerful blood did once atone,
And now it pleads before the throne.

- Isaac Watts
(1674–1748)

"Because Jesus is our great high priest, we've got a friend in high places. We've got connections in heaven. We've got a friend at the throne of grace who delights to answer our prayers. Come boldly. Come often. Come to the throne of grace and pour out your heart to God. You will not be turned away."[3]

– Ray Pritchard

*I am writing these things to you so that you may not sin.
But if anyone does sin, we have an advocate with the Father,
Jesus Christ the righteous.* (1 John 2:1)

In the American justice system, anyone accused of a crime has the right to legal representation. If the accused cannot afford to hire an attorney, the court system will appoint an advocate for him. An advocate is one who stands alongside another and appears on his behalf to plead his case.

Our defense attorney is Jesus. He advocates for us before the Father, applying to us the sufficiency of His sacrificial death. And as our Advocate, Jesus reconciles us to God and restores our fellowship with Him.

An attorney's job is to defend his client. No matter how serious the alleged crime or how obvious it appears to others that the defendant is guilty, the attorney is going to do everything possible to show that the defendant is not guilty; or, if he is proven guilty, to be sure that his client is not treated unjustly.

Jesus advocates for us in a different way. He knows we are guilty of breaking God's law, and He doesn't pretend that we're innocent. He always tells the truth, and the truth is that we are rebels. The reason He advocates for us is that justice has already been served. Those who have been justified in Christ can stand before God as if they had never sinned.

Yet we also have an accuser in this courtroom—Satan is a tireless prosecutor against God's children. He appears, at times, in the high court of heaven and before the throne of God, the righteous Judge. Satan brings charges against us, setting out our sins and failures and faults. When that happens, Jesus approaches the divine Judge and says, "This one has been fully pardoned. Justice has already been carried out, so let the prisoner go."

Because our sin has been reckoned to Jesus' account, and His righteousness has been imputed to us, we are guaranteed an acquittal. No accusation can stand against us in the courtroom of heaven if we are in Christ. "There is therefore now no condemnation for those who are in Christ Jesus" (Rom. 8:1).

The purpose of Jesus' first coming was to bring salvation, not judgment. But His second coming will be to bring eternal judgment on all who have not believed.

Is Jesus your Advocate? Have you trusted that your sins were placed on Him so that His righteousness could be credited to your account? If so, then you can rejoice that there is now no condemnation. And you can have great peace knowing that you don't have to fear the wrath of God and that nothing can make God love you less. Yes, we sin, but thanks be to God, we have an Advocate—Christ Jesus!

"Jesus defends those he died for, those who were his enemies. What a Savior that would pay for my crimes and, at the next turn, defend me as innocent! What accusation could stand up to that defense? None!"

~ Nick Bogardus

"[Jesus] did not simply live a perfect life and die on the cross for your sins. He still bears your burdens on his heart. He is still talking to God about you and for you. He is still pleading your case, still praying for your continued sanctification and your eventual glorification."[2]

- Robert Barnes

My Advocate appears
For my defense on High;
The Father bows His ears,
And lays His thunder by:
Not all that hell or sin can say
Shall turn His heart, His love away.

- Isaac Watts
(1674-1748)

Jesus, who intercedes for you at the throne of God, knows your heart and your need. On the basis of His atoning work on the cross, He offers His grace and forgiveness to cover your sins. Take time to express your gratitude to Him.

ALPHA AND OMEGA

And he said to me, "It is done! I am the Alpha and the Omega, the beginning and the end." (Revelation 21:6)

The apostle John was an old man when he was given a vision while in exile on the isle of Patmos. More than sixty years had passed since John had last seen the Lord Jesus, but in his vision, he was given a glimpse of things yet to come, and he heard Jesus say, "I am the Alpha and the Omega, the first and the last, the beginning and the end" (Rev. 22:13).

Alpha and omega are the first and last letters of the Greek alphabet; they represent the entirety of the alphabet. Jesus is the sum total of all of life. He is the God of beginnings and endings, of time and transitions.

He is in a class all His own. He was there at the beginning of time, and He'll be there at the end. He's the beginning and the end of all things, as well as everything in between. He is also the beginning and the end of our salvation. He is the author and finisher of our faith.

In packs of animals there is an alpha male, the dominant leader of the pack. Well, Jesus is the alpha being of the entire universe. "He is the beginning, the firstborn from the dead, that in everything he might be preeminent" (Col. 1:18).

By contrast, *"omega"* can refer to the last and the lowliest, and Christ made Himself low; He humbled Himself to the point of death on a cross. He is both Alpha and Omega.

The name also tells us that everything we need—peace, joy, help, grace, love, kindness—is found in Him. If it's not found in Him, we don't need it.

In Christ, we have the wonderful assurance that our lives are not left to chance. Every day and detail of our existence has been ordained by Him. So we can be free from fear. When we are faced with a scary, unknown future, we need to remind ourselves that Jesus is the first and the last, and that we can go forward, knowing that it's all wrapped up in Him.

To truly know Him is to be free from the cycle of worry that chronically pervades so many people's minds and emotions. Whatever our problems are, He is there. He holds us in the palm of His hand. He covers and surrounds us. Our trials, no matter how difficult they might be, are not the end of the story. Jesus is!

We live in a fallen, messed-up world, and bad things do happen. But regardless of what happens to us here on this earth, we can trust the Lord with our future. We know the end of the story—everlasting life with Him.

To know Jesus as the Alpha and Omega defines our calling, our purpose in life—He is our life, the Author and Finisher of our faith! We have no life apart from Him.

He wants to be "first and last" in your life—the first One you think about in the morning and the last One you think about as you lay your head on your pillow at night—the sum and circumference of your life.

"When Jesus says he is Alpha and Omega, he is saying, 'I am sufficient for everything; nothing is missing; I am all that you need.'"

~ Warren W. Wiersbe

"How certain are my expectations, and what suitable supplies of grace are assured to me in the interim, since he who is the Alpha and Omega of the universe, is also the author and finisher of my faith!"[2]

~ Rev. John East

Of the Father's love begotten,
Ere the worlds began to be,
He is Alpha and Omega,
He the source, the ending He,
Of the things that are,
That have been,
And that future years shall see,
Evermore and evermore!

~ Aurelius Prudenetius
(4th century poet)

Is Jesus the Alpha and the Omega of your life? Whatever you do—at work or home or church or out in the community—is He preeminent in your thoughts, affections, motives, words, and actions?

Since then we have a great high priest who has passed through the heavens, Jesus, the Son of God, let us hold fast our confession. HEBREWS 4:14

JESUS SERVES AS OUR GREAT HIGH PRIEST IN HEAVEN TODAY INTERCEDING AND ADVOCATING ON OUR BEHALF

The LORD roars from Zion . . . and the heavens and the earth quake.
But the LORD is a refuge to his people. (Joel 3:16)

A scroll with seven seals was shown to the apostle John in a vision he was given about the end of history. What John saw caused him great distress—there was no one able to break those seven seals and open the scroll.

But then John was told, "Weep no more; behold, the Lion of the tribe of Judah, the Root of David, has conquered, so that he can open the scroll and its seven seals" (Rev. 5:5). There is someone worthy after all. It is Jesus, the risen Savior.

Jesus alone has the authority to open the scroll that contains God's eternal purposes. He is able to prevail where others have failed. He is omnipotent where others are impotent. He is essential to the unfolding of God's eternal purposes. Lions are thought of as the king of beasts that rule the forest. Jesus is the Lion who rules the universe and all that happens in it.

John didn't actually see the Lion in his vision. What he saw instead was a slain Lamb. So is Jesus a lion, or is He a lamb? Lions and lambs are radically different. Lions are strong, lambs are weak. Lions are dangerous, lambs are harmless. Lions devour other animals, lambs are easily devoured.

The truth is, Jesus is both. He has supreme dominion over heaven and earth, yet He submitted to the cross. And He is worthy to open the scroll because He conquered sin through His atoning death. "Worthy are you to take the scroll and to open its seals, for you were slain, and by your blood you ransomed people for God from every tribe and language and people and nation" (v. 9).

The Lion's triumph was accomplished by His death

as a Lamb. He conquered by His suffering. And as the Lion of the tribe of Judah, Jesus is both the protector of His people and the prosecutor of His enemies. You will inevitably meet Him as one or the other. If you belong to Him, He will be as a Lion to defend and protect you, and anyone who tries to harm you will have to deal with Him.

Are there adversaries in your life, people who oppose Christ and give you trouble? They will have to deal with this Lion. Your enemies can make your life uncomfortable, but only for a while. At the final judgment, He will deal with those who have rejected Him, and all the world will tremble before Him.

And if we are children of God through faith in Jesus, we share in His victory. He triumphed by laying down His life, and we, too, will triumph as we take our place with Him, willing to be misunderstood and mistreated by the world for the time being. We conquer with Him by being willing to take up our cross and follow the slain Lamb.

Oh, that we would see and trust Him as the strong, powerful, courageous lion that He is!

O happy, happy tidings,
The kingdom now is opened.
The seals are all broken;
    Proclaim it afar;
From bondage and oppression
By Him we are delivered,
    The Lion of Judah,
    The bright Morning Star.

Hosanna in the highest,
All glory everlasting,
The cross and its banner
Triumphant shall wave;
Hosanna in the highest,
All glory everlasting,
    The Lion of Judah
    His people will save.

O the Lion of Judah hath triumphed forever,
O the Lion of Judah is mighty and strong.

- Fanny J. Crosby
(1820-1915)

"And now,' said Aslan presently, 'to business. I feel I am going to roar. You had better put your fingers in your ears.'

"And they did.... And they saw all the trees in front of him bend before the blast of his roaring as grass bends in a meadow before the wind."[1]

- C. S. Lewis
(1898-1963)

Does the thought of Jesus as a Lion comfort or distress you? Why?

*This is my beloved and this is my friend. . . .
I am my beloved's and my beloved is mine.* (Song of Songs 5:16; 6:3)

In the sixth day of creation there was a wedding. The first groom and the first bride were joined together. It was there that God established the institution of marriage, which was meant to be a picture of His heart toward His people. He loves them intensely—not a sappy, sentimental, Hollywood type of love, but one that's sacrificial, transforming, and redeeming.

Marriage is about far more than just human romance; it's about the romance of redemption. Ultimately, human marriage is meant to tell the story of God's plan to redeem His people by uniting them in marriage to His Son, the Bridegroom.

The apostle Paul makes this clear: "'Therefore a man shall leave his father and mother and hold fast to his wife, and the two shall become one flesh.' This mystery is profound, and I am saying that it refers to Christ and the church" (Eph. 5:31–32). Because of sin, that human picture is imperfect; nevertheless, earthly marriage is intended to showcase that divine marriage.

As a bridegroom woos a bride, Christ woos us. As a bridegroom rejoices when his chosen one accepts his proposal of marriage, Christ rejoices when we say yes to Him. As a bridegroom prepares a home in which to live with his wife, Christ prepares a place to take us to live forever with Him. As a groom pledges lifetime love to his bride, Christ says, "I will never leave you nor forsake you" (Heb. 13:5). As the groom gives the bride his name, Christ has given us His name. As the groom assumes responsibility to provide for his bride, Christ provides us with everything we need.

Our divine Bridegroom delights in being with His

bride. He shares His life with her, not just until someone better shows up or until she disappoints Him, but for the long term. This Bridegroom is jealous for His bride; He wants an exclusive, faithful relationship with her. If we allow worldly attractions to pull our hearts away, we commit spiritual adultery against our Bridegroom. It may be tempting at times to live as though we're "single," but if we belong to Jesus, we're already married!

Human marriage tells the story of Christ and His people, the Church, but it also foreshadows the ultimate marriage that will come at the end of time, when Jesus' steadfast love toward His people will be fully revealed. We don't yet have all that God has promised to us, so we look with faith and anticipation to that eternal marriage.

In the meantime, we are called to make ourselves ready for the wedding, for the Bridegroom's return. Our preparation is a response to His love and initiative. "It was granted her to clothe herself with fine linen, bright and pure'—for the fine linen is the righteous deeds of the saints. . . . 'Blessed are those who are invited to the marriage supper of the Lamb'" (Rev. 19:8–9). What a feast that will be for all eternity!

"The King of the universe came into the world to betroth to himself a bride at the price of his own blood. . . . He will come a second time to marry his bride and take us into the infinitely beautiful chambers and gardens of his love and joy forever. Everyone who trusts in Jesus belongs to that bride."[1]

– John Piper

"No husband loves the wife of his bosom, as much as Christ loved his people. . . . No husband is so undying and everlasting a husband as Christ is. . . . No bridegroom enriches his bride with such honors by marriage, as Christ does."[2]

– John Flavel
(1628–1691)

Hear the glad tidings, O Bride of the Bridegroom!
Rouse ye from slumber, the night is far gone;
Mystic in splendor, the morning star shineth,
    Heralding ever the nearing of dawn.

Sleeping or waking, redeemed ones together
Caught up the King in His beauty shall see!
Death with its sting, shall again threaten never;
    We like our Lord shall forevermore be.

~ Ford C. Ottman
(1859–1929)

Are you ready for the Bridegroom's return? If not, what do you need to do to get prepared?

*But of the Son he says, "Your throne, O God, is forever and ever,
the scepter of uprightness is the scepter of your kingdom." (Hebrews 1:8)*

When Jesus was on trial for His life, Pilate asked him, "Are you the King of the Jews?" To which Jesus responded, "You have said so."

As the trial unfolded, Jesus was rejected for His claim. Soldiers twisted together a crown of thorns and dressed Him in a purple robe. Crowns and robes belong to kings, but the people were not sincere in crowning Jesus. To the contrary, they mocked Him.

When Pilate said to the Jews, "Behold your King!" they cried out, "Crucify him!" And the religious leaders declared, "We have no king but Caesar." The people wanted a king, but Jesus was not the sort of king they wanted.

Pilate wrote an inscription and attached it to Jesus' cross. It read, "Jesus of Nazareth, the King of the Jews." The leaders objected and asked Pilate to change the wording to read, "This man said, I am King of the Jews." Pilate answered, "What I have written I have written."

Pilate got it right. Jesus is King, and there on the cross, the King of kings laid down His life for His subjects. One day that King will return. He came first as a suffering king, but when He comes back, He will rule forever from sea to sea.

Revelation 19 gives us a picture of our coming King: "His eyes are like a flame of fire, and on his head are many diadems" (v. 12). No longer will He wear a crown of thorns. He will be wearing the crown God gave Him when He was exalted as the King of kings.

"From his mouth comes a sharp sword with which to strike down the nations, and he will rule them with a rod of iron. He will tread the winepress of the fury of the wrath of God the Almighty. On his robe and on his thigh he has a name written, King of kings and Lord of lords" (vv. 15–16).

But that's not quite the end of the story. Satan and his minions and all those who resist God's reign and rule wage war against King Jesus. Eventually, those who lead rebellions against Christ as King are "thrown alive into the lake of fire that burns with sulfur" (v. 20). Other rebels are "slain by the sword that came from the mouth of him who was sitting on the horse, and all the birds [will be] gorged with their flesh" (v. 21). There is total devastation and ruin for all who refuse to bow before Jesus.

And in the end, King Jesus triumphs. He will have the final word over all other kings, over every human being, and over this entire world that He is redeeming and making new.

So are we going to try to rule our own lives, or will we let Jesus have His rightful place as King? If we resist His rule in our lives, we will lose. Those who willingly, gladly, wholeheartedly bow before Him will share in His ultimate, eternal triumph.

"He is King. It matters not that earth refused to crown Him and to acknowledge His right to reign. He only awaits the Father's day and hour to receive the kingdom which is His."[1]

– T. C. Horton &
Charles E. Hurlburt

"If Christ is the King, He deserves our honor, loyalty, and obedience."[2]

– Author unkown

The kingdom of this world
Is become the kingdom of our Lord,
And of His Christ;
And He shall reign forever and ever.

King of kings and Lord of lords!
Hallelujah!

–"Hallelujah" from
G. F. Handel's *Messiah*

Are there any areas of your life where you are trying to be your own king (finances, relationships, habits, values, etc.)? What do you have to gain by that strategy? What do you have to gain by bowing the knee to Christ as King?

I am writing these things to you so that you may not sin.
But if anyone does sin, we have an advocate with the Father,
Jesus Christ the righteous. 1 JOHN 2:1

No accusation can stand against us in the courtroom of Heaven if Christ is our Advocate

servant

Behold my servant, whom I uphold,
my chosen, in whom my soul delights. (Isaiah 42:1)

God's people, Israel, were called to serve the Lord, but they failed, and as a result, they became servants of their enemies. But God had planned for this. In His mercy and grace, He would send a righteous, ideal Servant to rescue them. The prophet Isaiah has much to say about this Servant.

God's perfect Servant would be gentle in how He dealt with people: "A bruised reed he will not break, and a faintly burning wick he will not quench" (Isa. 42:3). He would be tender with bruised and damaged lives. Some people seemed beyond repair, but the Servant of the Lord would repair and strengthen those lives and make them useful again.

Of course, Jesus, God's own Son, was this promised Servant. While on this earth, Jesus cared for the blind, the deaf, the lame, the lepers, the marginalized, the demonized, and the sexually promiscuous.

Isaiah foretold that this Servant would "not grow faint or be discouraged" (v. 4). He would not become weak, despondent, or disheartened. Instead, He would help despondent, broken people. He wouldn't give up until God's purposes were accomplished through Him, and in carrying out His mission, the Servant would suffer great injustice quietly—"he will not cry aloud or lift up his voice" (v. 2). Jesus did not raise His voice in His own defense. He sought justice for others, but He never demanded it for Himself.

"Though he was in the form of God, [he] did not count equality with God a thing to be grasped, but emptied himself, by taking the form of a servant" (Phil. 2:6–7). Jesus willingly embraced this calling: "The Son of Man came not to be served but to serve, and to give his life as a ransom for many" (Matt. 20:28). Jesus came to do what Israel had failed to do.

We, too, have been chosen as servants of the Lord—to carry out His purposes in the world. But we, too, have failed to be the servants we ought to have been. We are consumed with getting our personal needs met. So often we would rather be served than serve. We are reluctant to lay down our lives when it's inconvenient or costly. Yes, we have failed, but Jesus is the righteous substitute for the failed servant. He succeeded where we have failed.

Isaiah 52:13 tells us, "Behold, my servant shall act wisely; he shall be high and lifted up, and shall be exalted." God's Servant stooped down. He obeyed the Father and came to earth to serve fallen creatures who should have been the servants.

The exalted King became the humble Servant! He set aside His crown and His royal robes to serve us. If He had not done so, we would have no hope. But He did come, and He served. He stooped down and washed the feet of those who should have been servants in order to raise us up. Shall we not with grateful hearts forever delight to serve Him in turn?

What is an appropriate response to the fact that the Creator of the universe stooped down and became a humble servant of His creatures—that Jesus perfectly fulfilled the servant role we failed to fulfill?

"It is thrilling to know that when all others failed, Christ stepped down from His throne of splendor to 'stand in the gap' for a lost world."[1]

– Ivor Powell

"Like Jesus, we too are servants, servants of a new covenant (2 Cor. 3:6)—upheld by God, chosen by God, delighted in by God, empowered by his Spirit, called in righteousness, held by his hand and watched over by his eyes to bring forth justice to the nations and establish it in the earth."[2]

– Scott Grant

Servant of all, to toil for man
Thou didst not, Lord, refuse;
Thy majesty did not disdain
To be employed for us.

– Charles Wesley
(1707-1788)

Man of Sorrows

*Surely he has borne our griefs and carried our sorrows . . . .
It was the will of the LORD to crush him; he has put him to grief* (Isaiah 53:4, 10)

Heaviness and sorrow are inescapably and universally part of the human condition. Ultimately, all pain and suffering are the result of sin, whether our personal sin or someone else's. Sin always leads to sorrow, as Scripture makes clear, and mankind is not alone in experiencing the consequences. All of creation groans in pain. Worst of all, God sorrows. He experiences grief and sorrow over the sin of the human race.

God's grief is multifaceted. He grieves because His holiness has been assaulted, and He grieves over the broken relationship with His creatures. He's pained when those He loves so dearly resist His love and rebel against Him. God experiences deep, personal heartache over the effects of sin on His whole creation.

So with a grieving heart, God does two things. First,

in response to sin He sends judgment—He punishes. And second, He grants mercy and grace—He saves. God's grief over sin and the sorrow it causes led Him to send His Son, Jesus, to bear all this suffering. Jesus "was despised and rejected by men; a man of sorrows and acquainted with grief" (Isa. 53:3). The One who had known unmitigated joy for eternity past came to earth to become the Man of Sorrows.

As a boy, Jesus was misunderstood by His parents. During His earthly ministry, His brothers didn't believe in Him. He experienced hunger, exhaustion, and temptation. As the Man of Sorrows, He witnessed the ravages of sin in a broken world—sickness, death, grief, pride, prejudice, and hatred. He wept at the grave of His friend Lazarus. He wept over Jerusalem for her rejection of her Savior. He wept in the garden as He prepared to go to the cross and endure the ultimate suffering. This Man of Sorrows was betrayed, mocked, beaten, and crucified.

As we "survey the wondrous cross," we must ask ourselves, since the Father willed that Jesus should bear such sorrow and grief, how can we love the sin that caused it?

Much of the sorrow that abounds in the world is readily visible, but there is also much private pain that most never see. Yet Jesus has always seen, and He cared enough to do something about it. He drank the full cup of sorrow and pain that every person in the world through all of history has deserved. He is our Wounded Healer.

At the cross, judgment and salvation met so we could receive forgiveness, comfort, and healing. One day, every sorrow of those who have placed their faith in Him will be turned to joy. On the eve of the cross, Jesus said to His disciples, "You have sorrow now, but I will see you again, and your hearts will rejoice, and no one will take your joy from you" (John 16:22).

Man of Sorrows! what a name
For the Son of God, who came
Ruined sinners to reclaim.
Hallelujah! What a Savior!

– Philip P. Bliss
(1838–1876)

"The Lord exchanged the highest seat of heavenly honor for the lowest state of earthly humiliation and identified Himself with human sorrow in order to remove its very cause."

– Charles J. Rolls

"Although Jesus became the Man of Sorrows, He never lost sight of the fact that His sufferings were temporal; His joy would be eternal. He embraced our darkness that we who already live in the shadow of death might enter into a realm where darkness, sorrow, and death are unknown."[2]

– Ivor Powell

"Whatever your sorrows or trials may be —he knows by experience, how to sympathize with you."[3]

– Edward Payson
(1783–1827)

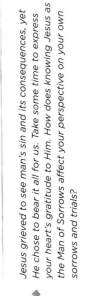

Jesus grieved to see man's sin and its consequences, yet He chose to bear it all for us. Take some time to express your heart's gratitude to Him. How does knowing Jesus as the Man of Sorrows affect your perspective on your own sorrows and trials?

Redeemer

*In him we have redemption through his blood, the forgiveness of our trespasses,
according to the riches of his grace. (Ephesians 1:7)*

From the first chapter of Genesis to the last chapter of Revelation, the Bible is a drama of redemption. Redemption is about deliverance. It speaks of rescue, release, and recovery. It's a word of hope in the midst of seemingly hopeless circumstances.

When your situation is dark and there appears to be no light at the end of the tunnel, redemption promises a brighter future ahead. When you can't dig yourself out of the hole of guilt and shame, redemption promises that your failure and the losses that have been caused by your sin can be overruled and you can be restored to usefulness.

But before we can be redeemed, we have to be desperate. We have to be in a predicament from which we cannot extricate ourselves.

And that is precisely our situation. We are trapped and cannot free ourselves from sin's vise. We need someone to reach out and help us. But there's a price to be paid. To redeem something means to buy it back for a price, a ransom.

In the days of the Old Testament judges, a widow named Naomi and her bereaved daughter-in-law, Ruth, were left without a provider, a future, or a hope. Their situation was bleak. But rescue came through Boaz, a kinsman-redeemer.

In those days, the next of kin was required to provide for a relative whose family name or lands were in jeopardy of being lost. A man had the duty when his brother died without children to take on the widow as his wife and to raise up children for his brother. This was all part of God's great redemptive story leading up to the line of Christ.

A kinsman-redeemer had to fulfill three qualifications,

all of which were fulfilled in Jesus. First, he had to be a relative. Jesus fulfilled this requirement when He took on flesh, and at the cross Jesus became sinners' nearest Kinsman by becoming sin for us.

Second, a kinsman-redeemer had to have the means to redeem. A poverty-stricken relative couldn't afford to help. And redemption was costly. It required personal sacrifice. Boaz was wealthy, so he had the ability to redeem Ruth and Naomi from their poverty. And Jesus had the means to redeem us—His own blood: "You were ransomed from the futile ways inherited from your forefathers, not with perishable things such as silver or gold, but with the precious blood of Christ, like that of a lamb without blemish or spot" (1 Pet. 1:18–19).

Finally, the kinsman-redeemer had to be willing to redeem. Aren't you glad Jesus wanted us?

Boaz fulfilled all three requirements and was able to redeem Naomi and Ruth, and Naomi was told, "Blessed be the LORD, who has not left you this day without a redeemer; and may his name be renowned in Israel!" (Ruth 4:14). That's a song every redeemed sinner can sing! There is a Redeemer; One who paid the price to win back all the losses occasioned by our sin, and He is our nearest Kinsman.

God's promised redemption, the One that prophets had foretold for hundreds of years, was fulfilled in Jesus Christ.

What has Christ redeemed you from? What does it mean to you in the present to have a Redeemer? In eternity?

"Redemption is the grand theme of the Bible; and Christ, the great Redeemer, is the right-royal subject of the entire volume."[1]

– Charles J. Rolls

O for a thousand tongues to sing
My great Redeemer's praise,
The glories of my God and King,
The triumphs of His grace.

– Charles Wesley
(1707–1788)

"We should feel the relief of rescue every day, for we have a Redeemer who bought us back."[2]

– Robert J. Morgan

Redeemed—how I love to proclaim it!
Redeemed by the blood of the Lamb;
Redeemed through His infinite mercy,
His child, and forever, I am.

– Fanny Crosby
(1820–1915)

Behold my servant, whom I uphold,
my chosen, in whom my soul delights. ISAIAH 42:1

THE·KING·
stooped
down
to save
His subjects
by sending
His Son
to earth as a
Servant.

For Christ, our Passover lamb, has been sacrificed. (1 Corinthians 5:7)

God came to Abraham and told him to take his beloved son Isaac and sacrifice him as a burnt offering. Abraham obeyed God. He got up early in the morning, cut wood for the offering, and headed out to make the sacrifice.

At the appointed place, Abraham put the wood on his son's back and took a knife and the fire to light the sacrifice. That's when Isaac said to his father, "Behold, the fire and the wood, but where is the lamb for a burnt offering?" Abraham answered, "God will provide for himself the lamb for a burnt offering, my son" (Gen. 22:7–8).

God did provide a substitute, foreshadowing that day when God would sacrifice His Son, the Lamb of God, who would die in our place.

Before Christ came, sacrificing lambs was a part of everyday life for the Israelites, which is why the words of John the Baptist were so significant: "Behold, the Lamb of God, who takes away the sin of the world!" (John 1:29). That was a stunning declaration to the Jews in that day, and it should be stunning to us because that sentence contains the heart of the gospel message.

The lamb symbolizes innocence, submission, vulnerability, quiet suffering, and sacrifice. The King of the universe came to earth as a gentle, sacrificial Lamb. Innocent and blameless, He suffered quietly for sins not His own. And He figures prominently in God's future and eternal plans for His people.

His sacrifice results in salvation for the people of God, but unrepentant sinners will be conquered by the wrath of the Lamb. This Lamb, who strikes terror in the hearts of unbelievers, strikes praise and worship in the hearts of those who have believed in Him. "Salvation belongs to our God who sits on the throne, and to the Lamb!" (Rev. 7:10).

One day you will face the Lamb, either as your Judge or as your Savior. Which will it be for you? Either He will conquer you, or you will be one of those who conquers with Him.

For all eternity the Lamb will have a relationship with those He died to save. "For the Lamb in the midst of the throne will be their shepherd, and he will guide them to springs of living water. . . . Let us rejoice and exult and give him the glory, for the marriage of the Lamb has come, and his Bride has made herself ready. . . . 'Blessed are those who are invited to the marriage supper of the Lamb'" (Rev. 7:17; 19:7, 9).

If you don't have a relationship with the Lamb in this life, you will not have one with Him in eternity; but if you do know Him personally, the Lamb will be your Shepherd and your Bridegroom forever.

Behold the Lamb. Trust the Lamb. Place your faith in Him who died to take away your sin, and worship the Lamb. Worshiping Him will be our eternal occupation in heaven. We will join the chorus of those who sing, "Worthy is the Lamb who was slain, to receive power and wealth and wisdom and might and honor and glory and blessing!" (Rev. 5:12).

It is so easy to take Jesus' sacrifice—the shedding of His blood—for granted. Remember again why the sacrifice was necessary. What is an appropriate response?

A Lamb goes uncomplaining forth,
The guilt of all men bearing;
And laden with the sins of earth,
None else the burden sharing!
Goes patient on, grow weak and faint,
To slaughter led without complaint,
That spotless life to offer;
Bears shame and stripes, and wounds and death,
Anguish and mockery, and saith,
"Willing all this I suffer."

This Lamb is Christ, the soul's great Friend,
The Lamb of God, our Savior;
Him God the Father chose to send
To gain for us His favor.
"Go forth, My Son," the Father saith,
"And free men from the fear of death,
From guilt and condemnation.
The wrath and stripes are hard to bear,
But by Thy Passion men shall share
The fruit of Thy salvation."

-Paul Gerhardt
(1607-1676)

"The day shall come when, from every place that God has made, there shall be heard the voice of praise unto the Lamb; there shall be found everywhere men and women redeemed by blood, angels and glorious spirits, rejoicing to adore Him who was, and is, and is to come, the Almighty Lamb of God."[1]

- C. H. Spurgeon
(1834-1892)

"The words of the Amen, the faithful and true witness." (Revelation 3:14)

Whatever you need, whatever your season of life, whatever your circumstance, whatever your challenge, whatever you may be facing this day, you will find all you need in the name of Jesus. He is worthy of all your trust and obedience, which is what the believers in the church at Laodicea had forgotten.

In Revelation there are letters to seven churches, and the one to Laodicea is the final letter. This church was in the worst spiritual condition of all seven, and Jesus has firm words for them. He begins by reminding those believers who He is: "The words of the Amen, the faithful and true witness, the beginning of God's creation" (Rev. 3:14). Jesus is the Amen, which means that He is constant and unchanging. This name fits Him perfectly. In fact, in its truest sense, it couldn't apply to anyone else.

He's the one who searches and inspects hearts. He knows the truth—He knows our true condition. He is about to tell the Laodicean church the truth about their condition, which is quite different from their perception of themselves. What about you? Do you trust His assessment of your true condition?

He is the Amen, the faithful and true witness. That means His words are trustworthy, and all His promises are true.

- He promises that if we seek the kingdom of God first, everything else we need will be added to us.
- He promises eternal life to all who believe in Him.
- He promises that those who ask will receive.
- He promises us a kingdom.
- He promises rest for our weary souls.

- He promises to come again and take us to be with Him forever.
- He promises that the gates of hell will not prevail against His Church.
- He promises that those who are willing to lose their life will find it.
- He promises His Spirit to guide and comfort us.
- He promises to be in the midst of His people who are gathered in His name.
- And He has promised, "I am with you always."

Jesus is the Amen, the faithful and true witness, so it behooves us to listen to what He says and to trust Him—His character, His promises, and His Word. He is worthy of your complete confidence. Whatever you may be going through, in every season and circumstance of life, you can cling to Him and count on Him.

Jesus is the guarantee of God's promises. Hebrews 1:1–2 says, "Long ago, at many times and in many ways, God spoke to our fathers by the prophets, but in these last days he has spoken to us by his Son." There is nothing else left to say. Our beloved Lord Jesus is God's final word, the Amen.

Believe Him, obey Him, heed Him, "for all the promises of God find their Yes [Amen] in Him. That is why it is through him that we utter our Amen to God for his glory" (2 Cor. 1:20).

What does it mean to you that Jesus is the Amen to all the promises and purposes of God? In our response to His promises, how can we "utter our Amen to God for his glory"?

"How do we know that God's Word is true and that we can stake our lives upon it? Jesus who lived, walked, died and rose among us is the great Amen. He is truly, truly the 'verily, verily.' He is the 'it is so' and the 'so be it' of God's promises."[1]

– William D. Watley

"The Amen is at the right hand of God, His word is sure and stable, every promise securely vested in Him; God has triumphed! 'Let us give unto the Lord the glory due to His Name.'"[2]

– F. A. Hughes

See the little baby, amen
Lyin' in a manger, amen
On Christmas morning
Amen, amen, amen!

See him in the garden, amen
Talkin' with the Father, amen
In deepest sorrow
Amen, amen, amen.

Led before Pilate, amen
Then they crucified him, amen
But he rose on Easter
Amen, amen, amen.

Hallelujah! Amen
He died to save us, amen
But he lives forever!
Amen, amen, amen!

– Jester Hairston
(1901–2000)

"The words of the Amen, the faithful and true witness." REVELATION 3:14

JESUS displays the faithfulness of God in fulfilling all His promises, His promises, He is God's final Word— the AMEN

Jesus

1 Kevin DeYoung, http://www.ligonier.org/learn/articles/the-name-of-jesus/

The Word

1 Ivor Powell, *Bible Names of Christ: 80 Names and Titles of Our Lord* (Grand Rapids, MI: Kregel Publications, 1988), 85.
2 Rubel Shelly, *The Names of Jesus: An In-Depth Exploration of the Christ,* (West Monroe, LA: Howard Publishing Co., 1999), 38.

Son of God

1 Henry Gariepy, *Portraits of Christ: Devotional Studies of the Names of Jesus* (Old Tappan, NJ: Fleming H. Revell Company, 1974), 80–81.
2 Charles J. Rolls, *The Name Above Every Name: Names and Titles of Jesus Christ, P–S* (Neptune, NJ: Loizeaux Brothers, 1965), 187.

Immanuel

1 Rubel Shelly, *The Names of Jesus: An In-Depth Exploration of the Christ,* (West Monroe, LA: Howard Publishing Co., 1999), 19–20.
2 *The C. H. Spurgeon Collection* (Ages Software) vol. 29, no. 1720. Found at http://www.spurgeongems.org/vols28-30/chs1720.pdf.

Wonderful Counselor

1 Warren W. Wiersbe, *The Names of Jesus* (Grand Rapids, MI: Baker Books, 1997), 34.
2 A. B. Simpson, *The Names of Christ* (Camp Hill, PA: Wing Spread Publishers, 1991), 5.
3 Karolina W. Sandell-Berg, "Day by Day," http://www.hymntime.com/tch/htm/d/a/y/daybyday.htm.

Mighty God

1 Warren W. Wiersbe, *The Names of Jesus* (Grand Rapids, MI: Baker Books, 1997), 47.
2 C. H. Spurgeon, "Zephaniah 3:17 The Savior Resting in His Love," no. 2720. Found at http://preceptaustin.wordpress.com/2013/06/19/jesus-might-god-el-gibbor/.

Prince of Peace

1 T. C. Horton, Charles E. Hurlburt, *Names of Christ,* ed. James S. Bell, Jr. (Chicago, IL: Moody Press, 1994), 121.
2 Robert J. Morgan, *He Shall Be Called: 150 Names of Jesus and What They Mean to You* (New York, NY: Time Warner Book Group, 2005), 220.
3 William Goode, *Essays on all the Scriptural Names and Titles of Christ, or the Economy of the Gospel Dispensation as exhibited in the Person, Character, and Offices of Christ, the Redeemer,* 6 vols. (London: L. B. Seeley and J. Hatchard and Son, 1822), vol. 3, 298.

Messiah

1 Henry Gariepy, *Portraits of Christ: Devotional Studies of the Names of Jesus* (Old Tappan, NJ: Fleming H. Revell Company, 1974), 187.
2 Horatius Bonar, "I Bless the Christ of God," http://cyberhymnal.org/htm/i/b/ibtcogod.htm.
3 William D. Watley, *Exalting the Names of Jesus* (Valley Forge, PA: Judson Press, 2002), 109.

Chief Cornerstone

1 Ivor Powell, *Bible Names of Christ: 80 Names and Titles of Our Lord* (Grand Rapids, MI: Kregel Publications, 1988) 40.
2 John MacArthur, "Christ: The Precious Cornerstone," http://808bo.wordpress.com/2013/07/04/john-macarthur-christ-the-precious-cornerstone/.

Captain

1 *Seasons of the Hearts: A Year of Devotions from One Generation of Women to Another,* compiled by Donna Kelderman (Grand Rapids: Reformation Heritage Books, 2013), November 9.
2 C. H. Spurgeon, "The Captain of our Salvation," *The C. H. Spurgeon Collection* (Ages Software, ver. 1.0) vol. 45, no. 2619. Found at http://www.spurgeongems.org/vols43-45/chs2619.pdf.
3 Isaac Watts, "Join All the Glorious Names," http://www.hymntime.com/tch/htm/j/o/i/joinatgn.htm.

Friend of Sinners

1 Alan Carr, "Jesus: The Friend of Sinners," http://www.sermonnotebook.org/new%20testament/Matt11_16-19.htm.
2 T. C. Horton and Charles E. Hurlburt, *Names of Christ,* ed. James S. Bell, Jr. (Chicago, IL: Moody Press, 1994), 75.

I AM

1 Charles J. Rolls, *The World's Greatest Names: Names and Titles of Jesus Christ, H–K,* revised edition (Neptune, NJ: Loizeaux Brothers, 1984), 77, 79.
2 T. C. Horton and Charles E. Hurlburt, *Names of Christ,* ed. James S. Bell, Jr. (Chicago, IL: Moody Press, 1994), 106.
3 Charitie Lees Bancroft, "Before the Throne of God Above," http://cyberhymnal.org/htm/b/e/beforetg.htm.

Bread of Life

1 Robert J. Morgan, *He Shall Be Called: 150 Names of Jesus and What They Mean to You* (New York, NY: Time Warner Book Group, 2005), 187.
2 Henry Gariepy, *Portraits of Christ: Devotional Studies of the Names of Jesus* (Old Tappan, NJ: Fleming H. Revell Company, 1974), 57.
3 Rev. Charles Terpstra, "I Am the Bread of Life," The Reformed Witness Hour, http://www.reformedwitnesshour.org/1997/1997sep14.html (September, 14, 1997).
4 John MacArthur, *The MacArthur New Testament Commentary: John 1-11* (Chicago, IL: Moody Publishers, 2006), 257.

Light of the World

1 Henry Gariepy, *Portraits of Christ: Devotional Studies of the Names of Jesus* (Old Tappan, NJ: Fleming H. Revell Company, 1974), 59.
2 John Piper, "I Am the Light of the World," Desiring God http://www.desiringgod.org/resource-library/sermons/i-am-the-light-of-the-world (March 12, 2011).

Good Shepherd

1 Robert J. Morgan, *He Shall Be Called: 150 Names of Jesus and What They Mean to You* (New York, NY: Time Warner Book Group, 2005), 244.
2 Chris Degner, "Follow Jesus, Our Shepherd-King," http://www.sermoncentral.com/sermons/follow-jesus-our-shepherd-king-charles-degner-sermon-on-jesus-teachings-60048.asp?Page=1 (July, 1994).

Resurrection and the Life

1 David Jeremiah, "In Search of Jesus . . . at the Tomb," http://www.crosswalk.com/1314225/.
2 J. N. Darby, "Jesus, the Resurrection and the Life," http://www.stempublishing.com/authors/darby/EVANGEL/12010E.html.

3 John Piper, "Jesus Is the Resurrection and the Life," *Desiring God*, http://www.desiringgod.org/resource-library/sermons/jesus-is-the-resurrection-and-the-life (September 17, 2011).

The Truth

1 Robert J. Morgan, *He Shall Be Called: 150 Names of Jesus and What They Mean to You* (New York, NY: Time Warner Book Group, 2005), 125.

2 Henry Gariepy, *Portraits of Christ: Devotional Studies of the Names of Jesus* (Old Tappan, NJ: Fleming H. Revell Company, 1974), 70.

3 William Mason, "The Lord Our Savior is the Way," http://www.hymntime.com/tch/htm/l/o/s/lositway.htm.

Savior

1 John Piper, "Why We Need a Savior," *Desiring God*, http://www.desiringgod.org/sermons/why-we-need-a-savior-dead-in-sins (December 8, 1985).

2 Charles Spurgeon, *Morning and Evening*, August 22, Evening, "The Unsearchable Riches of Christ," *Heartlight*, http://www.heartlight.org/spurgeon/0822-pm.html.

Lord

1 D. Martyn Lloyd-Jones, *Romans: Exposition of Chapter 10, Saving Faith* (Edinburgh: The Banner of Truth Trust, 1997), 94–99. Used by permission at http://www.teachingtheword.org/apps/articles/?articleid=702648&columnid=5435.

2 Ed Stetzer, "What It Means to Preach Jesus as Lord," http://www.sermoncentral.com/pastors-preaching-articles/ed-stetzer-what-it-means-to-preach-jesus-as-lord-1452.asp (December 10, 2012).

3 A. W. Tozer, "Submitting to Christ's Lordship," *The Alliance*, http://www.cmalliance.org/devotions/tozer?id=993 (August 1, 2013).

Head

1 Website introduction to John MacArthur, "Jesus, the Head of the Church," *Ligonier Ministries*, http://www.ligonier.org/learn/conferences/orlando_2006_national_conference/jesus-the-head-of-the-church/?gclid=Clug5_Xkk77kCFSpyQgod2BIACA.

2 C. H. Spurgeon, "The Head of the Church," *The C. H. Spurgeon Collection* (Ages Software) vol. 14, no. 839. Found at http://www.spurgeongems.org/vols13-15/chs839.pdf.

Great High Priest

1 John Piper, "Jesus: From Melchizedek to Eternal Savior, Hebrews 7:1–15," http://www.desiringgod.org/resource-library/sermons/jesus-from-melchizedek-to-eternal-savior (December 1, 1996).

2 T. C. Horton, Charles E. Hurlburt, *Names of Christ*, ed. James S. Bell, Jr. (Chicago, IL: Moody Press, 1994), 139.

3 Dr. Ray Prichard, "Great High Priest," http://www.crosswalk.com/blogs/dr-ray-prichard/great-high-priest.html.

Advocate

1 Nick Bogardus, "Jesus Is Our Advocate," http://marshill.com/2012/04/02/jesus-is-our-advocate (April 2, 2012).

2 Robert Barnes, "Jesus Is My Lawyer," *IIIM Magazine Online*, vol. 5, no. 28 http://thirdmill.org/newfiles/rob_barnes/nt.barnes.1john2.lawyer.pdf (July 19–26, 2003).

Alpha and Omega

1 Warren W. Wiersbe, *The Names of Jesus* (Grand Rapids, MI: Baker Books, 1997), 114.

2 Rev. John East, *My Savior: 52 Weekly Devotionals on the Names of Christ* (Timeless Christian Classics, 2009), 15–16.

Lion

1 C. S. Lewis, *The Lion, the Witch, and the Wardrobe: The Chronicles of Narnia* (New York, NY: HarperCollins Publishers, 2001), 185.

Bridegroom

1 John Piper, "Jesus Christ, the Bridegroom, Past and Future," *Desiring God*, http://www.desiringgod.org/resource-library/sermons/jesus-christ-the-bridegroom-past-and-future (April 4, 2004).

2 John Flavel, "Christ Altogether Lovely," *Fire and Ice: Puritan and Reformed Writings*, http://www.puritansermons.com/sermons/flavel1.htm.

King

1 T. C. Horton and Charles E. Hurlburt, *Names of Christ*, ed. James S. Bell, Jr. (Chicago, IL: Moody Press, 1994), 61.

2 "Jesus Is King," *The Word in Life Study Bible* (Nashville, TN: Thomas Nelson Publishers, 1993), 18–19.

Servant of the Lord

1 Ivor Powell, *Bible Names of Christ: 80 Names and Titles of Our Lord* (Grand Rapids, MI: Kregel Publications, 1988), 45.

2 Scott Grant, "The Servant of Compassion," http://www.pbc.org/system/message_files/10553/Is42-1-9.html (February 13, 2000). Copyright © 2000 Discovery Publishing, a ministry of Peninsula Bible Church.

Man of Sorrows

1 Charles J. Rolls, *Time's Noblest Name: Names and Titles of Jesus Christ, L–O* (Neptune, NJ: Loizeaux Brothers, 1985), 65.

2 Ivor Powell, *Bible Names of Christ: 80 Names and Titles of Our Lord* (Grand Rapids, MI: Kregel Publications, 1988), 48.

3 Edward Payson, "Christ, a Man of Sorrows," *Grace Gems!* http://www.gracegems.org/E/christ_a_man_of_sorrows.htm.

Redeemer

1 Charles J. Rolls, *The Name Above Every Name: Names and Titles of Jesus Christ, P–S* (Neptune, NJ: Loizeaux Brothers, 1965), 118.

2 Robert J. Morgan, *He Shall Be Called: 150 Names of Jesus and What They Mean to You* (New York, NY: Time Warner Book Group, 2005), 140.

Lamb of God

1 C. H. Spurgeon, "The Lamb of God in Scripture," *The Spurgeon Archive*, http://www.spurgeon.org/sermons/2329.htm, no. 2329). Delivered at The Metropolitan Tabernacle, Newington (August 25, 1889).

Amen

1 William D. Watley, *Exalting The Names of Jesus* (Valley Forge, PA: Judson Press, 2002), 89.

2 F. A. Hughes, "Jesus, The Amen" *Precious Things Magazine* (STEM Publishing, Mar/Apr, 1972), http://www.stempublishing.com/authors/hughes/JESUSAMN.html.

Through its various outreaches and the teaching ministry of Nancy Leigh DeMoss,
Revive Our Hearts is calling women around the world to freedom, fullness, and fruitfulness in Christ.

Offering sound, biblical teaching and encouragement for women through . . .

Books & Resources Nancy's books, True Woman books, and a wide range of audio/video

Broadcasting Two daily, nationally syndicated broadcasts (Revive Our Hearts and Seeking Him with Nancy Leigh DeMoss) reaching some one million listeners a week

Events & Training True Woman Conferences and events designed to equip women's ministry leaders and pastors' wives

Internet ReviveOurHearts.com, TrueWoman.com, LiesYoungWomenBelieve.com, daily blogs, and a large, searchable collection of electronic resources for women in every season of life

Believing God for a grassroots movement of authentic revival and biblical womanhood . . . Encouraging women to:

- Discover and embrace God's design and mission for their lives
- Reflect the beauty and heart of Jesus Christ to their world
- Intentionally pass on the baton of Truth to the next generation
- Pray earnestly for an outpouring of God's Spirit in their families, churches, nation, and world

Visit us at **ReviveOurHearts.com**. We'd love to hear from you!